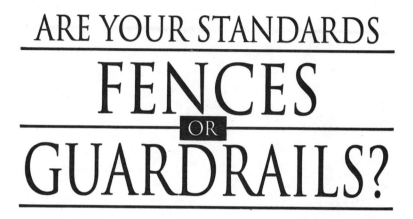

ARE YOUR STANDARDS
FENCES
OR
GUARDRAILS?

JOHN BYTHEWAY

DESERET
BOOK

SALT LAKE CITY, UTAH

Library of Congress Cataloging-in-Publication Data

Bytheway, John, 1962-
    Are your standards fences or guardrails? / John Bytheway.
      p. cm.
    Summary: Examines LDS Church standards related to movies, music, modesty, and morality, the principles behind the standards, and the peace that comes from living the standards.
    Includes bibliographical references and index.
    ISBN 1-57008-990-6 (pbk.)
    1. Mormon youth—Religious life.   2. Christian life—Mormon authors.
3. Church of Jesus Christ of Latter-day Saints—Doctrines.   [1. Church of Jesus Christ of Latter-day Saints.   2. Mormon Church.   3. Christian life.] I. Title.
    BX8643.Y6B95 2003
    241'.049332—dc22   2003012207

Printed in the United States of America   8006-7105
Banta, Menasha, WI

10 9 8 7 6 5 4 3 2 1

To all the LDS teenagers who go out and change the world every
day instead of letting the world change them

ACKNOWLEDGMENTS

I appreciate everyone at Deseret Book who helped put this book together, especially Michael Morris and Emily Watts for their help in preparing the manuscript for publication, Shauna Gibby for the cover and interior design, and Tonya Facemyer for the typesetting. Thanks always to Sheri Dew for her encouragement and advice.

I am indebted to Sue Egan, Irene Ericksen, Alvin W. Jones III, Barbara Barrington Jones, Joy Saunders Lundberg, Rand Packer, Jan Pinborough, Kirk Tenney, Brad Wilcox, S. Michael Wilcox, and Randal Wright for their writings and teachings, which have contributed to this book.

Special thanks to my wife, Kimberly, and also to my three children, who provide us with endless chaos, entertainment, and housework.

Normal books start with a table of contents. But this book is not normal. (And neither are you.) This book begins with a quiz. You'll probably ace it. Ready?

STANDARDS QUIZ

1. The Church has produced a pamphlet on standards for youth. It is called:

A. Standards for Youth.

B. Choose the Right.

C. For the Strength of the Youth.

D. Choose the Right When Convenient.

E. None of the above.

2. The purpose of standards is to:

A. Limit your freedom.

B. Control you.

C. Irritate you.

D. Protect you from consequences.

3. You want to go to a movie with your friends. What is the movie standard outlined by the First Presidency?

A. Don't see R-rated movies.

B. Don't see R- or PG-13-rated movies.

C. Don't see movies that are vulgar, immoral, violent, or pornographic in any way.

D. Only watch movies that are consistent with the thirteenth article of faith.

E. Immorality is acceptable as long as the movie makes you cry.

4. *You've got cash, and you want some new CDs. What is the music standard outlined by the First Presidency?*

A. Don't listen to music that degrades, enslaves, and binds your spirit.

B. Don't listen to music that drives away the Spirit, encourages immorality, glorifies violence, uses foul or offensive language, promotes Satanism or other evil practices.

C. Don't listen to music that is condemned by Oprah, Sally, Springer, or other noted theologians.

D. Listen only to music that is consistent with the thirteenth article of faith.

5. *You need a dress for junior prom. What is the dress standard outlined by the First Presidency?*

A. "Dress modestly" is the only guideline given.

B. Avoid strapless or spaghetti-strap dresses.

C. Avoid clothing that does not cover the shoulder, is low-cut in front or back, or is revealing in any other manner.

D. There is no specific guideline.

E. Only wear fashions approved by *Seventeen* magazine.

6. *You are about to turn sixteen. What is the dating standard outlined by the First Presidency?*

A. Date only Church members, go on group or double dates, and don't date before you're sixteen.

B. Date only those who have high standards and in whose company you can maintain your standards, and don't date before you're sixteen.

C. Sit down with your parents and set your own standards.

D. There are no specific guidelines other than to "choose wisely" and "bridle your passions."

E. Set standards based on popular TV shows named after zip codes.

7. You are old enough to date. What are the standards about physical affection outlined by the First Presidency?

A. Always treat your date with respect.

B. Stay in areas of safety where you can easily control your physical feelings.

C. Do not participate in talk or activities that arouse sexual feelings.

D. Do not participate in passionate kissing, lie on top of another person, or touch the private, sacred parts of another person's body, with or without clothing.

E. All of the above.

QUIZ ANSWERS AND TABLE OF CONTENTS

FOR A SICK WORLD, TAKE EXTRA-STRENGTH YOUTH

1. The Church produced a pamphlet on standards for youth. It is called:

    A. Standards for Youth

    B. Choose the Right

    C. For the Strength of the Youth

    D. Choose the Right When Convenient

    E. None of the above

The correct answer is E: None of the above. Answer C, "For the Strength of the Youth," is incorrect. The pamphlet is called *For the Strength of Youth*. (Okay, it was a trick question.)

FILL 'ER UP

Sometimes the most important topics are the most difficult to write about. In order for us to communicate, you and I both need to do our part. I'll try to write clearly, and I'd like you to try to read with an open heart. In fact, I'd like you to read with an open *jug*. Elder Bruce R. McConkie said:

1

We come into these congregations, and sometimes a speaker brings a jug of living water that has in it many gallons. And when he pours it out on the congregation, all the members have brought is a single cup and so that's all they take away. Or maybe they have their hands over the cups, and they don't get anything to speak of ("The Seven Deadly Heresies," *BYU 1980 Devotional Speeches of the Year* [Provo, Utah: Brigham Young University Press, 1981], 80).

I was a teenager when I first heard that quote, and I thought, "Why would you put your hand over the cup?" Since then, I've spoken at a few standards nights. When subjects like movies, music, or modest prom dresses come up, sometimes there's a bit of squirming among a few in the congregation. The expression on their faces seems to say, "Don't tell me I can't listen to my music." Or "Wait, don't tell me I can't see those kinds of movies." Or "Hey, this is supposed to be Church. The last thing I want is advice on how to be happy." They respond as if they are putting their hands over their cups.

I have a lot of information I'd like to share with you. You might say I have a jugful. My goal is that you will have a jugful when we're through. Most important, I hope the Spirit of the Lord will touch your heart when we talk about things that are right and true and good. So please listen with an open jug. And if something comes up that's hard to hear, please keep listening, and don't put your hand over the top.

AMEN TO THAT

As I mentioned above, I've had the opportunity to speak at a few standards nights. To be honest, standards are not my favorite subject, although they are critical to your happiness. But whether I'm talking about standards, the Book of Mormon, the Young Women values, or the duties of the Aaronic Priesthood, I always end my talks the same way: "In the name of Jesus Christ, amen."

Have you ever thought about what that means? It's a pretty bold statement. When we close in the name of Jesus Christ, it's like we're saying, "And what I've just said is what the Savior would say if he were here" or, at the least, "What I've said is worthy of the Savior's name."

Let's say I came to speak in your ward. For my talk to be worthy of the Savior's name, I'd have to give my message to you straight. I couldn't be concerned about whether you liked me or not because of the things I would say. I couldn't soft-pedal certain issues about movies or body piercing or modesty because someone might be uncomfortable. If I held back because of the "fear of men," or if I just gave you my own opinion about things, then I'd have no right to close my talk "in the name of Jesus Christ." And you wouldn't want me to tiptoe around the tough issues anyway, would you? Why would you want to listen to a fireside or read a book that didn't give it to you straight and undiluted? That would be a waste of time. Let me illustrate with another quiz question.

To have the endorsement of the Spirit of the Lord, what must a fireside, presentation, or book about standards contain?

A. The author's opinion of what the standards ought to be.

B. Your summer camp counselor's opinion of what the standards ought to be.

C. The opinion of active LDS young men and young women of what the standards ought to be.

D. Statements from the Lord and his servants on what the standards are.

Obviously, the answer is D (as in "duh"). We're not concerned about *who* is right (answers A, B, and C). We're concerned about *what* is right (answer D). And the only way we can enjoy the endorsement of the Spirit is if we share what the Lord and his servants have said.

THE STANDARD ANSWER

I've probably never been to your ward or stake center, and I doubt I've ever visited your high school gym or the arena where your favorite basketball team plays, but I know something about all those places. If I took a measuring tape and measured the height of the rim on the basketball standard, it would be ten feet above the floor. I know that's true because that's the standard. Whether it's a basketball court in high school, college, or the NBA, the rim is ten feet high. That's why we call them basketball *standards* rather than basketball *variables*.

When someone speaks in church, the bishop uses a little switch to adjust the height of the pulpit. If the speaker is tall, the pulpit goes up. If the speaker is short, the pulpit goes down. Basketball standards are different. We don't move the basketball standard up and down based on the height of the player with the ball. Try to imagine the chaos that would cause: "Yao Ming's got the ball, move it up!" BZZZZZZZZZ. "Oh no, John Stockton stole the ball, move it down!" BZZZZZZZZZ. The guy at the switch would have quite a headache at the end of the game. We don't look up at our basketball standards and say, "Hey, you have to adjust yourself to where I am!" Instead, we realize that we must adjust ourselves to the standard. We call our scriptures the "standard works" for the same reason. We can't just rip out certain pages to make the standard works adjust to us; we must adjust ourselves to the standard works. They are the standard by which we live, the standard by which we judge, and the standard by which we can find real happiness.

Perhaps you've heard the story of the man who was quite eager to talk to the Lord after he died and went to heaven. "Do you know what's going on down there?" the man asked. "There's hatred and crime and drugs and war and immorality—why didn't you send help?" The Lord answered, "I did send help. I sent you."

Today it's your turn. You've been sent to this world to help.

You can either change the world or let the world change you. You can either follow worldly fad and fashion or create a style of your own. To complete your mission, you're going to need to be strong. In fact, our world is so sick that it needs a dose of *extra-strength youth*.

But where do you get the strength you need to live the Lord's standards and to make a difference in today's world? Well, for Zion's youth in latter days, "truth gives [you] strength to dare" (*Hymns of The Church of Jesus Christ of Latter-day Saints* [Salt Lake City: The Church of Jesus Christ of Latter-day Saints, 1985], no. 256). And we know where to get the truth. It's right here, in the gospel of Jesus Christ.

WHY STANDARDS?

2. The purpose of standards is to:

    A. Limit your freedom.

    B. Control you.

    C. Irritate you.

    D. Protect you from consequences.

    The correct answer is D.

ON PURPOSE

What's the purpose of standards anyway? Well, I think we all know that they're really meant to limit freedom. Uptight parents invented standards to irritate teenagers and to make sure they don't have any fun. Right? Wrong. The purpose of standards is not to limit freedom but to *protect us from consequences of bad decisions* (Brent Barlow, *Worth Waiting For* [Salt Lake City: Deseret Book, 1995], 81–82). Smart mountain bikers wear helmets. Helmets are uncomfortable, they're hot, and they mess up your hair. But they protect you from consequences if your head should suddenly meet the mountain.

Loving parents are interested in protecting their children. One of my toddlers has a strange fascination with the dishwasher. She loves to reach into the silverware tray, grab a utensil, and take off running. If I find her waddling around the house with a paring knife, should I stand back and say, "Well, she has her agency," or "I don't want to limit her freedom"? What if she falls down on the knife because I didn't say "No!" and didn't take the knife away? Who would go to jail for being a lousy parent? I would. Why? Because a loving parent would have protected her. A loving parent would have said, "No!"

I'm crazy about my kids, and I tell them "No!" every day. They might think I don't want them to have any fun, but that's not the case. I tell them "No!" because of my great love for them. I care enough to draw lines and set boundaries. To limit their freedom? No! To protect them from consequences.

MAKE LIKE A TREE AND LEAF

Suppose you work for a landscaping company and have an assignment to cut down a tree. And let's say after a few hours, all you do is bring your boss a bag full of leaves. He might say you missed the point. Most of the tree is still there! There's more to trees than just leaves. Here's another example. Let's say I was trying to describe a tree to someone who had never seen one. If all I did was talk about leaves, I'd be leaving out most of the tree, *wood* I not? (Ha ha.)

The fact is, rules don't just float in midair. Rules are like leaves. They are supported by branches, which are supported by a strong trunk and sturdy roots. Branches are like *principles,* and the trunk and roots are like *doctrines.* For example, if I repeat the counsel that wherever possible the young men of the Aaronic Priesthood should wear a white shirt and tie while passing the sacrament, all I've done is explain the rule. But what's the principle that supports the rule? What's the branch? Good questions.

I believe that at least one of the principles supporting the rule about white shirts is *reverence*. We honor the Lord when we show reverence for sacred things like the sacrament. We wear white when we're baptized and when we go to the temple. Since white is a symbol for purity, we show reverence for the sacrament when we wear white (Jeffrey R. Holland, "This Do in Remembrance of Me," *Ensign,* November 1995, 68).

The *doctrine* behind the sacrament might be like the trunk and roots that support the rule. The sacrament reminds us of the sacrifice Jesus made for each of us, and it gives us a chance to renew our covenants. I am convinced that if all Aaronic Priesthood holders understood the *doctrine* of the atonement of Jesus Christ and the *principle* of reverence for sacred things, they would have absolutely no problem with the *rule.*

In the rest of this book, we'll talk about some rules. But the Church is much more than a long list of do's and don'ts, just as a tree is more than a bag of leaves. We'll talk about the rules, but we'll also point out the principles and doctrines that are at the root of the rules. I hope that as you read, you'll begin to recognize that there is a motive behind all the rules. The closer you look and the longer you ponder, the more you'll begin to recognize the plan of a loving Heavenly Father. He loves you so much that sometimes he says, "No." Other times he says, "Not yet." Why? To limit your freedom? No. To protect you from consequences—and to lead you to maximum happiness.

SOMEONE WANTS YOU TO SURRENDER YOUR SWORD

I noticed something interesting as I read the new *For the Strength of Youth* pamphlet. I saw the leaves and many of the branches, but the closer I read, the more I began to see the roots— the doctrines beneath every rule. The doctrines I noticed throughout the pamphlet have to do with a gift you received around your eighth birthday. This invisible gift is so powerful and so valuable that the Lord once called it "the unspeakable gift of the Holy Ghost" (D&C 121:26). It is a guide and a protection. In fact, it is a *weapon* to help you in this test of survival we call life.

What? The Holy Ghost is a weapon? *Yes.* You know the analogy—the "shield of faith," "the breastplate of righteousness," "the helmet of salvation," "loins girt about with truth," "and feet shod with . . . the gospel of peace" (D&C 27:15–18; Ephesians 6:14–17). Now if you'll picture the warrior I just described, you'll notice that I left something out. What's missing? The warrior I described has only defensive armor. But with a *sword*—a *weapon*—that warrior can go into the world and fight back. Where will the warrior get a sword? God wouldn't send us into this violent world unarmed would he? No! He gave us a gift. He gave us a weapon. He gave us the "sword of the Spirit" (D&C 27:18). Yes, the Holy Ghost is a sword, a powerful weapon to help us fight back when the temptations and false ideas of the world surround us.

Here's the problem: *the enemy is after your sword.* Your sword is your main defense against this world, and the adversary wants you to disarm and surrender. Do you remember how vigorously the enemies of Joseph Smith tried to get the gold plates after he had received them from Moroni? Joseph said:

> The most strenuous exertions were used to get them from me. Every stratagem that could be invented was resorted to for that purpose. The persecution became more bitter and severe than before, and multitudes were on the alert continually to get them from me if possible. But by the wisdom of God, they remained safe in my hands (JS–H 1:60).

In the same way and with that same kind of vigor, Satan wants to take from us the protection that God has given us. He'll stop at nothing to get our sword. He wants us to get so immersed in the movies, music, media, and morality of the world that we fall asleep spiritually. He wants to give us a *pacifier,* put us to sleep with a *lullaby,* convince us that standards are no big deal, and then *cheat* us out of our swords and lead us *carefully* to hell. Do these words sound familiar? I'll bet they do. Perhaps they remind you of 2 Nephi 28:21: "And others will he pacify, and lull them away into carnal security, that they will say: All is well in Zion; yea, Zion prospereth, all is well—and thus the devil cheateth their souls, and leadeth them away carefully down to hell."

Since "no unclean thing can dwell with God" (1 Nephi 10:21), Satan tempts us to go to unclean areas where the Holy Spirit cannot enter. He wants us to visit places where we have to leave our sword at the door. Just imagine the ticket taker at the movie theater saying, "I'm sorry, you won't be able to keep that in here. You must surrender your sword." Once we're disarmed, another spirit, a "false spirit," moves in and begins to plot our overthrow.

> Behold, verily I say unto you, that there are many spirits which are false spirits, which have gone forth in the earth, deceiving the world. And also Satan hath sought to deceive you, that he might overthrow you (D&C 50:2–3).

Again, Satan wants us to fall asleep spiritually and to be lulled and pacified. Then he wants to take our sword, our gift of the Holy Ghost, and lead us carefully to hell. Without the Holy Ghost, we lose our extra strength, and strong things become weak.

> And they saw that they had become weak, like unto their brethren, the Lamanites, and that the Spirit of the Lord did no more preserve them; yea, it had withdrawn from them because the Spirit of the Lord doth not dwell in unholy temples (Helaman 4:24).

Without our sword, we become spiritual weaklings. How can we prepare to become valiant moms and dads and missionaries when we're swordless? Elder M. Russell Ballard, speaking primarily to the young men who are preparing to serve missions pointed out a vital thing missionaries need to learn:

> We need vibrant, thinking, passionate missionaries who know how to listen to and respond to the whisperings of the Holy Spirit. This isn't a time for spiritual weaklings. We cannot send you on a mission to be reactivated, reformed, or to receive a testimony. We just don't have time for that. We need you to be filled with "faith, hope, charity and love, with an eye single to the glory of God" (D&C 4:5) ("The Greatest Generation of Missionaries," *Ensign,* November 2002, 47).

SHOW AND TELL

We're blessed because in the gospel of Jesus Christ we have words *and* swords. The scriptures tell us how to live, and the companionship of the Spirit shows us what to do. "Feast upon the words of Christ; for behold, the words of Christ will *tell* you all things what ye should do. . . . and receive the Holy Ghost, it will *show* unto you all things what ye should do" (2 Nephi 32:3, 5; emphasis added). I'm glad you're reading this book. It shows that you are a thoughtful, sober-minded, amazing teenager. But you could read a hundred books on how to make choices, and none of them could match the value of the companionship of the Spirit. The scriptures tell, but the Spirit shows! Elder Richard G. Scott said:

> Have you discovered that detailed instructions on how to make choices, or how to live your life based on someone else's experiences, are not nearly as helpful as is personal guidance from the Holy Ghost? Such divine guidance comes from pondering and living the doctrines of the Lord, understanding His plan of happiness, and obtaining the ordinances and keeping the covenants central to that plan. Such a foundation allows the Holy Ghost to give you guidance and

direction, taking into consideration your personal strengths and needs. The promptings of the Holy Ghost will tell you how you stand before God, if you are progressing or retrogressing, what you need to improve on, and how to do it ("Have No Regrets," *Brigham Young University 1999–2000 Speeches* [Provo, Utah: BYU Publications, 2000], 17–18).

I hope you have good friends. The more time we spend with others, the more we become like them. Sometimes we even adopt their gestures and words. If that's true, we'd better be careful who we spend time with! What could we say about those whose constant companion is the Holy Ghost? Will they begin to become like God? Where will that association take them? President James E. Faust has taught:

> I testify that as we mature spiritually under the guidance of the Holy Ghost, our sense of personal worth, of belonging, and of identity increases. I further testify that I would rather have every person enjoy the Spirit of the Holy Ghost than any other association, for they will be led by that Spirit to light and truth and pure intelligence, which can carry them back into the presence of God (*Reach Up for the Light* [Salt Lake City: Deseret Book, 1990], 123).

This book will make much more sense as you recognize the importance of the Holy Ghost in your life. It is priceless. It is unspeakable. When we sing, "Lead me, guide me, walk beside me" (*Hymns,* 301), we must realize that much of that guidance comes from the Holy Ghost. We must also realize that there is another spirit out there who is not holy—a cunning spirit who wants to lead you to spiritual death. We are enticed by both, but only we can decide which Spirit to follow.

> O, my beloved brethren, remember the awfulness in transgressing against that Holy God, and also the awfulness

of yielding to the enticings of that cunning one. Remember, to be carnally-minded is death, and to be spiritually-minded is life eternal (2 Nephi 9:39).

I guess the big question is, whose enticings will we follow? The Holy Ghost can bring us peace and happiness and lead us back into the presence of God. The evil spirit is determined to lead us and guide us "carefully down to hell," but first, he'll try to persuade us to surrender our sword. To protect us from the terrible consequences of following the evil spirit, the Lord and his servants have given us a wonderful protection: doctrines and principles and rules that will allow us to stay armed and prepared to do battle with the world—we call them standards.

MEDIA

3. You want to go to a movie with your friends. What is the movie standard outlined by the First Presidency?

A. Don't see R-rated movies.

B. Don't see R- or PG-13-rated movies.

C. Don't see movies that are vulgar, immoral, violent, or pornographic in any way.

D. Only watch movies that are consistent with the thirteenth article of faith.

E. Immorality is acceptable as long as the movie makes you cry.

The correct answer is C.

Some people think the answer is A: "Don't see R-rated movies." Why would they think that? Well, back in 1986 President Ezra Taft Benson said, "Don't see R-rated movies." That's not difficult to understand, but it presents a problem. What if you are a member of the Church who lives outside the United States? What if your country uses a different movie-rating system or doesn't have a rating system at all? Good question. The fact is, President

15

Benson said more (I didn't let him finish). Let's look at his whole quote: "Don't see R-rated movies or vulgar videos or participate in any entertainment that is immoral, suggestive, or pornographic" ("Youth of the Noble Birthright," *Ensign,* May 1986, 45).

Did you notice how important it is to read the entire sentence? Yes, President Benson said, "Don't see R-rated movies," but he also said to avoid *"any* entertainment" that can be described using these four adjectives: vulgar, immoral, suggestive, and pornographic. Are any PG-13 movies vulgar or immoral? Yup. Are any PG-13 movies suggestive and pornographic? Absolutely, and we all know it.

Four years after President Benson's talk, the Church published the 1990 version of *For the Strength of Youth.* Its counsel about movies used all four of President Benson's adjectives and added a new one. It also mentioned that we should not rely solely on movie ratings: "Don't attend or participate in any form of entertainment, including concerts, movies, and videocassettes, that is vulgar, immoral, inappropriate, suggestive, or pornographic in any way. Movie ratings do not always accurately reflect offensive content" (*For the Strength of Youth,* 11–12). A few years later, Elder H. Burke Peterson mentioned that R-rated movies aren't the only ones we shouldn't see.

> Stay away from any movie, video, publication, or music—*regardless of its rating*—where illicit behavior and expressions are a part of the action. Have the courage to turn it off in your living room. Throw the tapes and the publications in the garbage can, for that is where we keep garbage. . . .
>
> Again I say, leave it alone. Turn it off, walk away from it, burn it, erase it, destroy it. I know it is hard counsel we give when we say movies that are R-rated, and many with PG-13 ratings, are produced by satanic influences. Our standards should not be dictated by the rating system ("Touch

Not the Evil Gift, Nor the Unclean Thing," *Ensign,*
November 1993, 43).

In 2002 we received an updated *For the Strength of Youth*. The
standard for entertainment in the new edition uses four adjectives,
and one of them is new: "Do not attend, view, or participate in
entertainment that is vulgar, immoral, violent, or pornographic in
any way. Do not participate in entertainment that in any way presents immorality or violent behavior as acceptable" (*For the
Strength of Youth,* 17). Did you notice the new adjective?
"Violent." We'll come back to that in a moment.

If you ever hear someone say, "In our Church we're not supposed to see R-rated movies," you can say, "Actually, we're not
supposed to see any movies that are vulgar, immoral, violent, or
pornographic in any way, or movies that make violence and
immorality acceptable." Our standard is based on principles. It
works for Latter-day Saints in any country in the world, and
because it's based on true principles, it will never have to be
updated.

I'd like to answer a question that may have come up in your
mind: "Brother Bytheway, why did the *For the Strength of Youth*
pamphlet change? I thought you just said that standards don't
change?" That's right. The rules might be worded differently, but
the principles and doctrines have not changed. Do you know what
changed? The world did—dramatically. I'll explain:

MAYBERRY IS MY HOMETOWN

I have a rather strange hobby. I absolutely love *The Andy
Griffith Show*. In case you've never heard of it, it's an old black
and white comedy about a sheriff named Andy; his son, Opie; his
Aunt Bea; and his deputy, Barney Fife. It all takes place in a small
town called Mayberry. I have taped about two hundred episodes,
and when my wife and I decide there's nothing good on TV
(which is just about every time we turn it on), we throw in a tape

and go to Mayberry. *The Andy Griffith Show* first aired in 1960. It was the top show on television when they stopped making new episodes in 1968, and it has never been off the air since.

One day while browsing through Church books at Deseret Industries, I found a *For the Strength of Youth* pamphlet that was published way back in 1965, right in the middle of the *Andy Griffith Show* era. The entire highly illustrated pamphlet was only sixteen pages long. Twenty-five years later when the Church produced an updated *For the Strength of Youth* pamphlet, it was nineteen pages long with no illustrations. The newest *For the Strength of Youth* is—get this—forty-three pages long.

Why the big change? Are there new commandments that we didn't have before? Is the Church just adding more and more rules? No. The fact is, the moral standard from 1965 to 2002 is exactly the same. It hasn't changed one bit. The world, however, is quite different. The new *For the Strength of Youth* addresses topics that didn't need to be addressed in the days of *Andy Griffith*— a day when the number one show on television depicted family members who loved one another, went to church each week, said their prayers at night, and never used curse words.

Today the popular television shows either avoid religion or ridicule it. They mock the law of chastity in nearly every episode, and they use language that never would have been heard on the air in 1965. Some people call that progress. I think it's more like decay.

I've watched about one hundred hours of the Andy Griffith show, and in those one hundred hours I cannot find one curse word. Not one instance of sex outside of marriage, not even one innuendo (a joke that refers to immorality). Not one in one hundred hours! I defy anyone to find any episode of *Friends* without all those things—sometimes in the first scene! Yup, things have changed.

THE EARTH WAS FILLED WITH VIOLENCE

You see, the standard hasn't changed, but the world has. Remember the new word we noticed in the latest *For the Strength of Youth?* The word was "violent." It's an interesting word. Think back for a moment to Noah's ark and the flood. Think of what was happening on the earth before the rains fell. Why was the earth flooded? Because the people were wicked, right? Right. But that isn't the word the scriptures use. They use a different word:

> The earth also was corrupt before God, and the earth was filled with *violence.* And God looked upon the earth, and, behold, it was corrupt; for all flesh had corrupted his way upon the earth.
>
> And God said unto Noah, the end of all flesh is come before me; for the earth is filled with *violence* through them; and, behold, I will destroy them with the earth (Genesis 6:11–13; emphasis added).

The earth was flooded and the wicked destroyed because the world was corrupt and filled with violence. Our movies and TV shows are also filled with corruption and violence. Things are so bad these days that we even put ratings on computer games. Do you think the leaders of the Church know about violent computer games and what they can do to your spirit?

In a recent general conference, Elder M. Russell Ballard suggested that we can prepare to serve the Lord by "limiting the amount of time spent playing computer games. How many kills you can make in a minute with a computer game will have zero effect on your capacity to be a good missionary" ("The Greatest Generation of Missionaries," *Ensign,* November 2002, 46).

Everything from movies to video games is filled with violence, and perhaps that's why the standards now use the word "violent" when describing the entertainment we should avoid.

I'LL WATCH IT, BUT IT
DOESN'T MEAN I'LL ACT THAT WAY

One LDS young woman mentioned to her grandpa that she'd recently seen the movie *Titanic*. Her grandpa said, "Didn't that movie have some immorality in it?" His granddaughter replied, "Yeah, but they were so in love." I can only imagine what this grandpa said next.

When we learn things in the gospel, or when the Holy Ghost instructs us, we often describe that kind of learning as "line upon line, precept upon precept" (2 Nephi 28:30; D&C 98:12). I believe that Satan has an evil counterfeit for just about everything, and I believe he likes to get us to watch certain TV shows and movies so he can teach us "lie upon lie, and decept upon decept."

In fact, someone once said that Satan will tell ten truths if he can fit in one lie. For example, a movie may feature terrific acting, a fantastic script, stunning visual effects, a gorgeous soundtrack, and a story that tugs at your heartstrings and makes you cry. But its message may be, "It's okay to break the law of chastity if you're really in love." That's the message the young woman above came away with. And she is not just an ordinary young woman. She is a young woman who, every week with her class, says, "We will stand as witnesses of God at all times, in all things, and in all places as we strive to live the Young Women Values. . . ."

Satan is persuasive, he is relentless, and he is very patient.

BUT I KNOW LOTS OF PEOPLE
WHO WATCH EVERY NEW MOVIE

So do I. But we're not talking about *who's* right; we're talking about *what's* right. Some people like to argue that President Benson's quote and *For the Strength of Youth* are only for teenagers. Oh, puh-leeese. In other words, adults don't need the gift of the Holy Ghost? Is there a double standard? There's a scary verse in the Bible that says some of the very elect could be deceived in the last days (Matthew 24:24). Could our attitudes about today's entertainment prove that we've already been deceived? Elder J. Richard Clarke taught:

> There is only one standard of moral decency. Any film, television show, music, or printed material unfit for youth is also unfit for parents. Those who rationalize acceptance of immoral material on grounds of maturity or sophistication *are deceived*. Those who excuse transgression by saying "Well, I'm not perfect" may be reminded that conscious sin is a long way from perfection ("'To Honor the Priesthood,'" *Ensign,* May 1991, 42; emphasis added).

The older and more mature you become, the more you will govern your life by *principle* rather than by *example*. When a four-year-old gets scolded for doing something wrong, he might point at someone else and say, "Well, he did it. Why can't I?" He's governing his actions by example. You normally won't hear a four-year-old say, "Mom, today in nursery Matthew stole Chelsea's fishy crackers, but I just couldn't participate—it's the principle of the thing." Also, you probably won't see a grown man point at someone else and say, "Well, he did it. Why can't I?" But you might hear him say, "Well, I realize that many people do that, but I choose not to. It's the principle of the thing."

Unfortunately, you may know some adults who see movies they probably shouldn't see. Sure, you could excuse your personal behavior because of their example, but the Lord is asking you to be wise enough and mature enough to govern your life by what is right, not by what is popular.

I UNDERSTAND THE RULE,
BUT I DON'T UNDERSTAND THE WHY

This is a good place to remember that rules are like leaves, branches are like principles, and trunks are like doctrines. Let's look at the rule, the principle, and the doctrine on page seventeen of *For the Strength of Youth*:

The Rule: *Do not attend, view, or participate in entertainment that is vulgar, immoral, violent, or pornographic in any way. Do not participate in entertainment that in any way presents immorality or violent behavior as acceptable.*

So here's the question: Why shouldn't I see movies like that? We could probably come up with lots of answers. Because it's bad. Because by watching, we participate in bad behavior. Because we've been asked not to. Because we don't want to support an industry that makes bad stuff. All of those responses are correct, but more important than what happens to the industry is what happens to you. Now let's look for the principle or the branch that supports the leaf.

The Principle: *Whatever you read, listen to, or look at has an effect on you. Therefore, choose only entertainment and media that uplift you.*

Now we're getting somewhere. Everything you do has a consequence. Everything you watch has an effect on you! Now let's keep reading, and we'll discover the doctrine.

The Doctrine: *Good entertainment will help you to have good thoughts and make righteous choices. It will allow you to enjoy yourself without losing the Spirit of the Lord.*

Bingo! There's the doctrine. Good entertainment allows you to keep your sword—the Holy Ghost. You will find that the entire *For the Strength of Youth* pamphlet was written to help you keep your gift of the Holy Ghost. It's your defense and your weapon of protection as you go out and face the world.

I suspect that if we wanted to restate the rule about movies and entertainment, we could say it just like this: "Don't participate in entertainment that offends the Spirit of the Lord." Someone might ask (and someone probably has), "But what offends the Spirit?" We could answer with the rule: "If it is vulgar, immoral, violent, or pornographic, and if it presents immoral or violent behavior as acceptable, then it offends the Spirit and causes the Spirit to withdraw."

Another doctrine in which the standards are rooted deals with the fact that God is *holy*. The Spirit is often called the *Holy* Ghost or the *Holy* Spirit. Holy means pure and good. God wants us to be holy too, so he gave us the gift of the Holy Ghost to be our companion. The Holy Ghost will lead us to things that are good and pure and steer us away from things that are not. The Holy Ghost will help us to "stand . . . in holy places, and be not moved" (D&C 87:8).

If something is holy, it will build you spiritually. I'll bet you've heard someone call your meetinghouse or stake center an *edifice*. An edifice is a building, and when something builds us spiritually, we say, "That was edifying," or "I was edified."

Here's another great scripture to remember when making your decisions about movies, television, and Internet sites. "And that which doth not edify is not of God, and is darkness." If it doesn't build you spiritually, then God had nothing to do with it. The scripture continues, "That which is of God is light. . . . And I say it that you may know the truth, that you may chase darkness from among you" (D&C 50:23–25). I love that. It doesn't say "avoid dark things" or "don't partake." It says we should *"chase darkness from among [us]."* Imagine if we could all have that attitude about movies and media and if we could all unsheathe our swords and chase away the bad while screaming, "Get off my turf and out of my sight!"

WHY DOESN'T THE CHURCH MAKE A LIST OF WHAT MOVIES ARE ACCEPTABLE?

I don't think the Church wants to hire anybody to watch movies all day (although I know people who would love to apply for the job). Besides, every week so many new movies arrive at the theater and come out on video and DVD that they can hardly be numbered. So you have to learn to decide on your own what to allow into your mind.

Worldly things can get into your head in a couple of different ways—through your eyes and through your ears. Movies do both. What we see and hear affects our *thoughts,* and our thoughts become our *words* and our *deeds.* That's true today, and it was true in Book of Mormon times. I wonder if King Benjamin's people asked him a question like the one above—not about a list of bad movies but perhaps about a list of all the different ways they could commit sin. Maybe that's why King Benjamin said:

> And finally, I cannot tell you all the things whereby ye may commit sin; for there are divers ways and means, even so many that I cannot number them. But this much I can tell you, that if ye do not watch yourselves, and your words, and your deeds, and observe the commandments of God, and continue in the faith of what ye have heard concerning the coming of our Lord, even unto the end of your lives, ye must perish. And now, O man, remember, and perish not (Mosiah 4:29–30).

The way the rules are stated puts you in charge of making decisions. You are responsible for your own behavior, so you must decide. You wouldn't learn and grow much if the Church told you what to do every second of every day. Instead, the Church is interested in teaching correct principles, allowing you to "study it out in your mind" (D&C 9:8) and then make your own choice.

Joseph Smith was once asked how he managed to govern so

many people and keep things in such good order. He did *not* say, "I tell them what to do every second." Instead, he responded, "I teach them correct principles, and they govern themselves" (*Messages of the First Presidency,* comp. James R. Clark, 6 vols. [Salt Lake City: Bookcraft, 1965–75], 3:54).

So the reason the Church doesn't make a list of which movies, television shows, and videos are acceptable is simple: the Church offers us something even better. It teaches us correct principles that will help us make every decision, and these correct principles will never need to be updated. With the advent of the Internet, we have another way to get movie reviews before we pay our money. We can find out ahead of time if a movie meets the standard simply by checking out online reviews, such as those found at www.screenit.com.

SATAN'S SMART BOMBS

Recently I wrote a book about honoring the Aaronic Priesthood. I asked several young men in my ward to read the manuscript before I sent it to the publisher. One chapter mentioned the dangers of pornography, and one of the deacons who reviewed the manuscript wrote in the margin, "What's that?" I'm so glad he didn't know.

Simply put, pornography is explicit pictures, which include movies, TV shows, magazines, or Internet sites that are intended to cause sexual arousal. Pornography is very dangerous stuff, and Satan uses it as one of his deadliest weapons. In fact, Satan has developed "advanced weapon systems" for his war against chastity and virtue. I'll explain.

I love airplanes. Ever since I was as young as I can remember, I've looked into the sky with excitement whenever an airplane flew overhead. I built dozens of model airplanes before my teenage years, and when I was in college I took flying lessons and soloed in a Cessna 152. I loved flying the Cessna, but I've always wanted to have my own F-16. I don't want to bomb anyone; I would just love to have something grossly overpowered. Airplanes are sleek and beautiful, and it's unfortunate that they're often used for destructive purposes.

Many years ago, I noticed a chart in an issue of *U.S. News and World Report* that fascinated me.

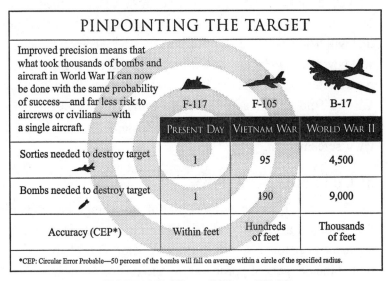

PINPOINTING THE TARGET			
Improved precision means that what took thousands of bombs and aircraft in World War II can now be done with the same probability of success—and far less risk to aircrews or civilians—with a single aircraft.	F-117	F-105	B-17
	PRESENT DAY	VIETNAM WAR	WORLD WAR II
Sorties needed to destroy target	1	95	4,500
Bombs needed to destroy target	1	190	9,000
Accuracy (CEP*)	Within feet	Hundreds of feet	Thousands of feet
*CEP: Circular Error Probable—50 percent of the bombs will fall on average within a circle of the specified radius.			

(*U.S. News & World Report*, 11 February 1991, 27)

The B-17 Flying Fortress had a crew of ten and was the primary bomber used in Europe during World War II. You'll notice that it took 4500 sorties (individual missions) and 9000 bombs to destroy a target. And the bombs they dropped were accurate to within "thousands of feet" of the target.

During the Vietnam War, many pilots flew the F-105 Thunderchief. Because of improvements in the technology of war, destroying a target required only 95 missions and 190 bombs—a huge improvement. And the bombs they dropped were accurate to within "hundreds of feet" of the target.

Then war technology improved again. In 1991 the F-117 Nighthawk stealth fighter was used during the Gulf War. Sorties required? Only one. Bombs required to destroy the target? One. And the accuracy was "within feet." In fact, the F-117's laser-guided weapons can be programmed to fly through a specific window of a building! Again, it's too bad that such beautiful things as airplanes often have to be used for such violent and destructive purposes, but there's a lesson in all of this that I want you to see.

War technology has improved, and *Satan is at war against us.* He'll use any weapon he can to try to kill us spiritually. During the days of World War II, those who wanted pornography had to go to a bad part of town. They probably had to travel "thousands of feet." They also had to ask for it, and they likely felt ashamed as they reached for their wallet.

Then the spiritual war technology improved. Guess what was invented during the Vietnam War? The VCR. Today you only need to go "hundreds of feet" to a supermarket, a convenience store, or a video/DVD rental place to find movies that are "vulgar, immoral, violent, or pornographic." For a few bucks you can bring these movies right into your home, the center of Satan's target. Satan uses the latest technology to teach us of his ways right from our own television. What furniture in your house shows the most wear? For most of us, it's the furniture facing the TV, or the "home entertainment center."

In the past two decades, technology has improved again. Today if you have unfiltered Internet access in your home, Satan can park a smart bomb right on your desk, "within feet" of where you're sitting. Those who produce pornography have been looking for a secret way into our homes, and they've found it. Satan can now target us with his most lethal weapons with pinpoint accuracy.

We can buy a security system for our house, we can put dead-bolt locks on each of the doors, and we can install motion sensor lights outside. Satan, however, can enter our homes through very small spaces. He can come through the cable, the modem, or even through the air (to your satellite dish).

SCRIPTURAL SHIELDS, PROPHETIC PROTECTIONS

We're under attack, as our prophets have continually told us. I've never heard stronger counsel from the leaders of the Church than their warnings about pornography. President Gordon B. Hinckley has spoken in very sobering terms about the destructive power of this modern weapon of Satan:

> Stay away from pornography! Avoid it as you would a terrible disease. It is a consuming disease. It is addictive. It gets hold of men and grasps them until they can scarcely let go. . . . These magazines, these video tapes, these late-night programs, you don't need them. They will just hurt you, they won't help you. They will destroy you, if you persist in looking at them (*Teachings of Gordon B. Hinckley* [Salt Lake City: Deseret Book, 1997], 463).

Of course, the Internet is not the only way pornography spreads. Elder Richard G. Scott mentioned six different delivery systems Satan uses to attack the world with this modern plague:

> One of the most damning influences on earth, one that has caused uncountable grief, suffering, heartache, and destroyed marriages is the onslaught of pornography in all of its vicious, corroding, destructive forms. Whether it is through the printed page, movies, television, obscene lyrics, the telephone, or on a flickering personal computer screen, pornography is overpoweringly addictive and severely damaging. This potent tool of Lucifer degrades the mind, the heart, and the soul of any who use it. All who are caught in its seductive, tantalizing web and remain so will become

addicted to its immoral, destructive influence ("The Sanctity of Womanhood," *Ensign,* May 2000, 37).

Now we know the rule. Don't get anywhere near pornography. It's too dangerous. The "maybe just a little won't hurt" attitude can be deadly because pornography is so addictive. Remember what Moroni said: "Touch not the evil gift, nor the unclean thing" (Moroni 10:30). He didn't say, "A little won't hurt," or "It's okay in moderation." He said, "Don't even touch it!" In the same verse, Moroni also encouraged us to "lay hold upon every good gift." We know exactly which gift to cling to—the gift of the Holy Ghost.

Earlier in this book when we talked about the standard for entertainment, we mentioned that the doctrine that supports the rule is to keep the Spirit of the Lord with you. Notice how quickly Jesus goes from the rule to the doctrine in this verse:

> And verily I say unto you, as I have said before, he that looketh on a woman to lust after her, or if any shall commit adultery in their hearts, they shall not have the Spirit, but shall deny the faith and shall fear (D&C 63:16).

The major consequence of touching the *evil* gift is the loss of the *holy* gift, or the gift of the Holy Ghost. It's amazing that on your eighth birthday, among all the gifts you received from your family and friends, you also received a gift from God. It didn't come in a package; it came through the priesthood. It's priceless and powerful. It's your sword! And if you start looking at evil gifts, you lose it. And your faith turns to doubt, and your doubt turns to fear.

IT'S THE THOUGHT THAT COUNTS

When George Albert Smith was a thirteen-year-old boy, he heard Karl G. Maeser, the principal of Brigham Young Academy, say, "Not only will you be held accountable for the things you do, but you will be held responsible for the very thoughts you think." This idea troubled the young student until he came to an important realization:

> Why, of course you will be held accountable for your thoughts, because when your life is completed in mortality, it will be the sum of your thoughts. That one suggestion has been a great blessing to me all my life, and it has enabled me upon many occasions to avoid thinking improperly, because I realize that I will be, when my life's labor is complete, the product of my thoughts (in Ezra Taft Benson, "Think on Christ," *Ensign,* April 1984, 10).

Usually, our thoughts are pretty random. They jump all over the place based on what's going on around us. But sometimes we deliberately put things into our minds. We do that when we choose to watch TV, buy movie tickets, rent videos, or visit Internet sites. That's when we have to be careful. The gospel encourages us to think our thoughts according to a plan. Imagine that! We're actually supposed to *plan* our thoughts! The apostle Paul taught:

> Finally, brethren, whatsoever things are true, whatsoever things are honest, whatsoever things are just, whatsoever things are pure, whatsoever things are lovely, whatsoever things are of good report; if there be any virtue, and if there be any praise, *think on these things* (Philippians 4:8; emphasis added).

At the judgment day, we will be "the sum of our thoughts." You've probably heard that we'll be judged according to our works and our desires, and that's true (Alma 41:3). But we think about things before we do them. Every action begins with a thought; therefore, our thoughts will either condemn us or bless us. Alma taught:

> For our words will condemn us, yea, all our works will condemn us; we shall not be found spotless; and our thoughts will also condemn us; and in this awful state we shall not dare to look up to our God; and we would fain be glad if we could command the rocks and the mountains to fall upon us to hide us from his presence (Alma 12:14).

Wow! I think that's just about the scariest verse I've ever read. But it's also a motivating verse because it makes us want to control our thoughts and channel them to things that are good and holy and noble and true. The question is, what do you think?

A FINAL THOUGHT

Now you know a little bit more about the standards. You know a little bit more about how we should choose our movies, videos, television shows, Internet sites, and even computer games. You know that we may have to sacrifice some of our . . .

Oops, hold everything. That's the wrong word. *Sacrifice* is when we give up something *good* for something *better.* Giving up entertainment that is vulgar, immoral, violent, or pornographic is not a sacrifice. What we're talking about is giving up something *bad* for something good. What would we call that? How about "being wise" or "receiving the truth" or "keeping our guide"?

> For they that are wise and have received the truth, and have taken the Holy Spirit for their guide, and have not been deceived—verily I say unto you, they shall not be hewn down and cast into the fire, but shall abide the day (D&C 45:57).

Phew, that was close. You've got to be careful how you use the word sacrifice. Saying "no thanks" to a lot of today's entertainment isn't a sacrifice; it's a pleasure.

I was born into an *Andy Griffith Show* world. You're growing up in a much different world. My *For the Strength of Youth* had sixteen pages. Yours has forty-three. When I was a teenager no one had movies in their home. Today people own hundreds of tapes and DVDs. You've been sent to do battle in a world that is much different than the world just a few decades ago. The world needs you. It's a good thing you're here, and it's a good thing you're armed. See you next chapter.

MUSIC

4. You've got cash, and you want some new CDs. What is the music standard outlined by the First Presidency?

A. Don't listen to music that degrades, enslaves, and binds your spirit.

B. Don't listen to music that drives away the Spirit, encourages immorality, glorifies violence, uses foul or offensive language, promotes Satanism or other evil practices.

C. Don't listen to music that is condemned by Oprah, Sally, Springer, or other noted theologians.

D. Listen only to music that is consistent with the thirteenth article of faith.

The correct answer is B.

Sometimes little kids say brilliant things. One day while running errands in the car, my wife turned on the car stereo and started searching for something to listen to. One of the songs we heard while surfing through radio stations was rather loud and obnoxious. My little girl suddenly made an insightful comment. She said, "That music sounds mad." I thought that was a pretty good description coming from a three-year-old. Some music sounds mad!

I read recently that teenagers spend between four and five hours a day listening to music or watching music videos and that listening to music is their preferred non-school activity. Much of today's popular music is full of anger, rage, and hopelessness. Hmmm, what do you suppose could happen to young people who fill their minds with anger, rage, and hopelessness for four to five hours a day? There's a chance they might become, well, full of anger, rage, and hopelessness. On the other hand, what do you suppose could happen to someone who listens to inspirational music or programs full of faith, hope, and testimony? I suppose they might become more faithful and hopeful, as well as stronger in their testimony.

If you've stayed with me this far, I suspect that you are a pretty impressive teenager. I suspect that you agree with what you've read up until now and that you're looking for reinforcement and encouragement in what you already believe. Good for you. As you know, music, like other media, is another way for good messages or bad messages to get into your head and into your spirit. Since the only gatekeeper for your ears and eyes is you, you have to be the one who stands guard to protect the doorway into your spirit. Lots of undesirable stuff wants to get in, and you're the only one who can check IDs at the door.

COMPACT DECEPTION

Imagine the devil having a meeting with his angels. "I have an idea," he might say. "I think we can get LDS teenagers to listen to CDs filled with crude expressions, vulgar stories, curse words, and violence. In fact, I think we can get them to listen to this stuff all day long. They'll become so addicted that they'll make headphones a part of their clothing and carry a stereo with them wherever they go! We'll pump this stuff into their brains constantly so that it affects everything they do, including the way they treat their family, the way they act at school, the way they feel—everything!"

The devil's angels might respond, "How will we get them to buy CDs with all that stuff on it?"

"Simple," the devil might reply. "We'll disguise it by putting it to music. The message we want them to hear will be in the lyrics, and if their parents complain, they'll say, 'I don't see what's wrong with this,' or 'C'mon, Mom, it's just a song,' or 'I don't really listen to the lyrics.'"

As the one and only guard for the entryway into your spirit, you're the one who has to learn how to recognize who's trying to get inside. And beware—sometimes unwanted intruders will be in disguise.

A bishop told me once that his son came home from the mall with a bunch of CDs. The bishop didn't have to hear the music to know what it contained; he just looked at the covers. "Son," he said, "I want you to open these CDs and read the lyrics to each song. Then I'd like you to ask yourself what the message of each song on each CD is. When you're done, I'd like you to ask one more question: Are the messages on these CDs compatible with the message I'm trying to send the world as a holder of the priesthood?"

To the young man's credit, he took his father's assignment. He discovered that the messages in the lyrics and the message of the gospel were not compatible. In fact, they were nearly opposite, and he got rid of the CDs.

If all of the young men and young women in the Church could have the kind of courage this young man had, we really could produce what Elder M. Russell Ballard has called "the greatest generation of missionaries in the history of the Church" ("The Greatest Generation of Missionaries," *Ensign,* November 2002, 47). Would you be willing to try the same experiment with your CDs? Are you willing to go through your music and clean things up? We say that we seek after things that are "virtuous, lovely, or of good report or praiseworthy" (Articles of Faith 1:13). Well, do we, or is that just a saying? Have our headphones made us deaf to the whisperings of the Spirit?

PLANE TALK ABOUT MUSIC

A number of years ago, Elder Gene R. Cook of the Quorum of the Seventy boarded a flight from Mexico to Texas. As he often does while traveling, he introduced himself to the person sitting next to him by saying, "My name is Gene Cook. I'm a member of The Church of Jesus Christ of Latter-day Saints. What's your name?" The man next to him replied, "My name is Mick Jagger."

"Well, I'm glad to meet you, Mick," said Elder Cook. The man repeated, "I said, my name is Mick Jagger."

"I heard you, Mick," said Elder Cook. Mick Jagger then opened a magazine, pointed at his own picture, and said, "This is me."

At one point in the conversation, Elder Cook asked, "I have opportunity to be with the young people in many different places around the world, and some of them have told me that the kind of music that you sing, and others like you, has no effect on them— that it's okay, that it doesn't affect them adversely in any way. And others of the young people have told me that it has a real effect on them for evil, and that it affects them in a very bad way, very honestly. You've been in this business for a long time, Mick. I'd like to know your opinion. What do you think is the impact of your music on the young people?"

Mick Jagger replied, *"Our music is calculated to drive the kids to sex."*

Elder Cook said, "I must have had a real look of shock on my face." Mick Jagger then quickly added, "It's not my fault what they do; that's up to them. I'm just making a lot of money."

Elder Cook continued to explain that Mick Jagger felt that

"this was a great day for them [rock musicians] because now instead of just having audio, where they could portray whatever they wanted to about sex and all the rest, they now had videos and could show it and have the person hear it and see it portrayed." The result, Jagger added, is greater impact on the youth and greater wealth for him (*13 Lines of Defense: Living the Law of Chastity* [Salt Lake City: Deseret Book, 1991], audiocassette, side 3).

I am not familiar with the music of Mick Jagger and the Rolling Stones, and perhaps you aren't either. The reason I share this story is that I want you to ask yourself a couple of questions: If Mick Jagger has these ideas about his music, could there be others, perhaps many others, in the music industry who have similar motives? Could there be others who teach through their music that there's nothing wrong with immorality? If so, do you want to support their goals by giving them your money so that they can teach even more young people the same thing?

SAMUEL THE LAMANITE AT THE MALL

One day while reading the words of Samuel the Lamanite about the popular people of his day, I thought to myself, "Wow, this sounds like the way the world treats celebrities and rock stars!" Samuel the Lamanite said these words on top of a wall, but he could have said them at the mall. See if you agree:

> But behold, if a man shall come among you and shall say: Do this, and there is no iniquity; do that and ye shall not suffer; yea, he will say: Walk after the pride of your own hearts; yea, walk after the pride of your eyes, and do whatsoever your heart desireth—and if a man shall come among you and say this, ye will receive him. . . .
>
> Yea, ye will lift him up, and ye will give unto him of your substance; ye will give unto him of your gold, and of your silver, and ye will clothe him with costly apparel; and

because he speaketh flattering words unto you, and he saith
that all is well, then ye will not find fault with him.

O ye wicked and ye perverse generation; ye hardened
and ye stiffnecked people, how long will ye suppose that the
Lord will suffer you? Yea, how long will ye suffer yourselves
to be led by foolish and blind guides? Yea, how long will ye
choose darkness rather than light? (Helaman 13:27–29).

When it comes to music, our goal is to choose light. So we
want to choose music that allows the Spirit to remain with us.
When we listen to good music, the Holy Ghost can be our companion, and we won't have to surrender our sword and be led
around by our headphones—or by blind and foolish guides and
greedy music producers. Notice again the music standard on page
fourteen in *For the Strength of Youth:*

> Choose carefully the music you listen to. Pay attention to
> how you feel when you are listening. Don't listen to music
> that drives away the Spirit, encourages immorality, glorifies
> violence, uses foul or offensive language, promotes Satanism
> or other evil practices.

I have to admit that I was a little shocked when I first heard
the story about Mick Jagger and Elder Gene R. Cook. I expected
Mick Jagger to say, "Well, we may sing about it, but it doesn't
mean they'll do it." But that's not what he said. His specifically
said, "Our music is *calculated* to drive the kids to sex."

For music or any other form of media to *drive* you to commit
some kind of sin, something else has to happen first—the Spirit
has to leave you. Apparently, many people in this world want to
drive the Spirit of the Lord out of you so that they can then *drive*
you into sins and habits that will destroy you. That should *drive*
us crazy. Some young people are being led so carefully that they
don't even see what's happening. That's scary.

Author S. Michael Wilcox has shared the story of a young

woman in his institute class. She was a talented singer who got a job singing with a rock band. At first, she didn't see what was wrong with her new environment. She explained:

> My parents were greatly distressed that I was using my talents, which they had helped me develop through music lessons, with music they felt was harmful. However, I thought they were just old-fashioned and were condemning something they knew nothing about. I joined a rock band. Even though I was uncomfortable at first with the environments we sang in and the clothing I was asked to wear, in time I adjusted and felt fine.
>
> Everyone but me could tell how much I was changing, but I convinced myself that the clothing was just a costume and that the lyrics were only words. I really liked a group who produced some very hard music. I had placed posters of their lead singer all over my room, much to the despair of my mother in particular. One night after a concert, I came home, turned the light on in my room, and stared at the poster of my favorite rock singer. He had on a pair of black leather pants. He was chained as if he were a prisoner with a look of pain on his face. Suddenly, I felt as if the Savior entered my room, stood beside me, and looked at the poster with me. I think the Lord gave me a great gift, because I felt so ashamed. There was nothing desirable in the poster. I saw the whole rock industry for what it was. I tore down the poster, removed all other signs of rock from my room, and put up an old picture of the Savior I'd had when I was a Mia Maid (*Don't Leap with the Sheep* [Salt Lake City: Deseret Book, 2001], 55–56).

I love music. I have *always* loved music. I play the guitar, and I'm learning the banjo and the piano. I'm really good at the CD player too. I'll bet I have a few hundred CDs at home. I have music that makes me feel energetic (music I listen to when I'm jogging), and I have music that makes me feel reverent. I have music that makes me feel happy, music that makes me feel sad, and music that reminds me of the first time I met my wife.

I am grateful that we belong to a Church that cares what we let into our eyes and ears. It's just more evidence that there is a God in heaven who loves us, who wants the best for us, and who sometimes says "No" because he cares about us.

It's time to ask ourselves some tough questions. Are we willing to go through our CDs and toss out the ones with messages that don't match the message we've been sent to earth to deliver? Can we imagine the Savior standing by our bed, looking at the posters in our room?

The gospel is not for spiritual wimps. As someone once said, if we don't stand for something, we'll fall for anything. Fortunately, we are not wimps. We are armored, and we are armed.

Once again, we've noticed something: Keeping the Spirit, or living in such a way that we can "always have his Spirit to be with us," is the ultimate purpose of the standard. It's the doctrine that supports the rule.

MODESTY

5. You need a dress for junior prom. (Note: Boys, you do *not* need a dress for junior prom—let's make that clear.) *What is the dress standard outlined by the First Presidency?*

    A. "Dress modestly" is the only guideline given.

    B. Avoid strapless or spaghetti-strap dresses.

    C. Avoid clothing that does not cover the shoulder, is low-cut in front or back, or is revealing in any other manner.

    D. There is no specific guideline.

    E. Wear only fashions approved by *Seventeen* magazine.

The answer is C. (Guys, you may think the following chapter was written for young women only. However, I'd like you to read it too, and pay close attention to the part about tattoos, body piercing, and other extreme fashions).

This chapter will be a little harder for me to write than the others. For one thing, I'm not a teenager any more, and for another thing, I've never worn a prom dress in my life. We just had certain rules at my house. In fact, I'm quite sure none of my friends in the priests quorum ever wore prom dresses. I think the entire ward was grateful for that. None of us looked very good in pink chiffon anyway. We tried it once for our ward basketball uniforms, and it just wasn't our color.

I believe it's easy for most young people to understand why listening to bad music, watching bad movies or TV shows, or viewing bad Internet sites would offend the Spirit. What is harder to understand is how our choice of what we *wear* can offend the Spirit. I'll do my best to explain.

I still remember how interesting it was to be a new missionary in the Missionary Training Center and see what other missionaries wore on preparation day. On "P-day" we took our dress shirts to the laundry and wore casual clothes. Suddenly I discovered things about the other missionaries I didn't know when we all arrived in our white shirts and ties. When one missionary in our district walked into the laundry room, I immediately thought, "Oh, he's a cowboy." Another walked in wearing camouflage army fatigues, and I thought "Oh, ROTC." They probably looked at me when I walked in and said, "Oh, city boy" or, perhaps, "Oh, how sad."

Anyway, my point is that clothes communicate who we are and even what we believe. Imagine if we sent our missionaries out wearing torn, faded jeans and tie-dyed shirts instead of dress pants, classy white shirts, and neckties? What if their noses or ears were pierced and their hair were spiked? What if they looked sloppy instead of sharp? Do you think they'd get in as many doors? Do you think they'd have the chance to share the gospel message with as many people? No way. Their fashion message would get in the way.

What missionaries wear sends a message about who they are and what they believe. Can I say that again? (Of course I can, I'm the author.) *What they wear sends a message about who they are and what they believe.*

A NOT SO SECRET MESSAGE

What message are *you* trying to send? When you walk the halls at your high school, what do people think about you from the way you dress? When you make your grand entrance at the prom, what would you rather have people think: "Wow, doesn't she look classy" or "Hey, we already have a Britney Spears"?

As you and I were baptized, we made a covenant. We promised to "stand as witnesses of God at all times and in all things, and in all places" (Mosiah 18:9). We might also add the phrase, "and in all prom dresses" (Carol B. Thomas, "Spiritual Power of Our Baptism," *Ensign,* May 1999, 93). We can either look like the world or stand out from the world. The fact is, when we were baptized we were taken out of the world and placed in the kingdom of God on earth. Therefore, as members of God's kingdom, we ought to dress and act and behave like children of the King.

What we wear doesn't just send a message, it *is* a message, and that message either qualifies for the Spirit or it doesn't. It's nice when your shirt and pants match, but as members of the Church, we have to make sure the clothes on our bodies match the testimony in our spirit.

> Your dress and grooming send messages about you to others and influence the way you and others act. When you are well groomed and modestly dressed, you invite the companionship of the Spirit and can exercise a good influence on those around you. Never lower your dress standards for any occasion. Doing so sends the message that you are using your body to get attention and approval and that modesty is important only when it is convenient (*For the Strength of Youth,* 15).

You may think that others shouldn't make assumptions about people based on their clothes, but they do. If you dress scantily, others might assume your morals are scant as well. If you wear revealing clothes, you may also be revealing your attitude about modesty and virtue. More important, if you dress like the world, the message you send is worldly, and the Spirit cannot accompany worldly things. What exactly is a "worldly" look? I'm glad you asked:

> Immodest clothing includes short shorts and skirts, tight clothing, shirts that do not cover the stomach, and other revealing attire. Young women should wear clothing that covers the shoulder and avoid clothing that is low-cut in the front or the back or revealing in any other manner. Young men should also maintain modesty in their appearance. All should avoid extremes in clothing, appearance, and hairstyle. Always be neat and clean and avoid being sloppy or inappropriately casual in dress, grooming, and manners. Ask yourself, "Would I feel comfortable with my appearance if I were in the Lord's presence?" *(For the Strength of Youth, 15–16).*

The fact is, very few people really need immodesty spelled out with such detail. We all know what it is.

PROM AND CIRCUMSTANCE

I have a friend named Sue Egan who told me something that happened to her when she served as a stake Young Women president. As her children were preparing to go to the junior prom, a large group of young men and young women gathered at her home to drive to the dance together. Being a Young Women leader and a hyper mom, she said to the girls, "Come in and show me your prom dresses!"

(Can you imagine a Young Men president doing the same thing? "Hey, guys, come in and show me your tuxedos! Okay, now twirl around. Say, that's a stylin' cummerbund!" Guys and girls are different—I'm glad.)

One by one the girls walked into the middle of the room,

twirled around, and did whatever else you do at a fashion show. Everyone gushed and flowed with compliments as each girl stepped out. Finally it was the last girl's turn to show her dress. Sister Egan didn't intend to embarrass anyone, but the last girl in line didn't walk out. She was lingering in the back of the room for a reason. Her dress did not meet the standard, and she knew it. She finally walked into the room with her head down and her arms crossed in front of her. Her conscience told her she should hide the front of her dress and cover her low neckline.

Sister Egan didn't know what to do. She didn't have to say anything, however, because the girl's dress was immodest, and everyone knew it, including the girl.

Years earlier, when Sister Egan was a younger woman, she was walking north on Main Street in Salt Lake City. Ahead of her a few tourists had stopped on the sidewalk to look through the fence located east of the Salt Lake Temple. As they were watching newlywed couples get their pictures taken, an old man suddenly turned the corner and started walking southbound on Main Street. The tourists noticed him for a moment and then looked back at the newlyweds. Sister Egan thought to herself, "I guess they don't know who that is—that's President Kimball."

When Sister Egan faced her closet that morning, she could have worn anything she wanted. She had no idea whom she might bump into that day. When she met the prophet by accident, she was so glad that she didn't have to look down at the ground with her arms crossed in front of her.

Let's say that the gym floor at your school is being refinished, and your school has to hold junior prom at a large convention center. And let's say that one of your friends discovers that President Hinckley is talking to the press in an adjacent room. Now let's imagine that your friend runs to you and says, "Let's go meet him!" Here's a bold question: Could you do it? Would you feel comfortable meeting the president of the Church in your last prom dress? Good. I thought so.

Some young women might be thinking, "Brother Bytheway, you have no idea how hard it is to find a modest prom dress." They're right. Like I said before, I've never worn a prom dress. In fact, I've never even shopped for one. But if Nephi were here, he might say, "I see your point. And you have no idea how hard it is to get brass plates from a man who is trying to kill you. I had to hike two hundred miles in a desert, and you may need to drive twenty miles in air-conditioned comfort."

When it comes to buying a prom dress, you have a chance to show your true colors. You can respond as Nephi's brothers did: "It is a hard thing which [you] have required of [us]" (1 Nephi 3:5). Or you can respond as Nephi did: "I will go and do the things which the Lord hath commanded" (1 Nephi 3:7).

BUT I WANT TO BE ATTRACTIVE!

Of course you should dress to be attractive, but attractive doesn't mean provocative. You don't want to look like someone with loose morals or like someone who worships her own body. You want others to value you for you, not for how you look. The world speaks in superficial terms about people. Hollywood is interested in "the look" or "the image," and that's about it. I have a friend who was a former Miss Utah (she's now a mom with four kids). She told me that she made many friends while competing in the Miss America pageant, and she knows a lot of young women who later appeared on the front cover of fashion magazines. Guess where they are now?

They're gone. Why? Because they got older. Hollywood and fashion magazines used them for a while and then threw them aside. Why? Because they were nothing but marketing tools for cosmetics. When they got older, they became obsolete. Because the world values a "look" and an "image" and doesn't care a bit about what you are on the inside. In the same way, if you're only concerned about your look, some boys may want to take you to a dance but only as a trophy on their arm. They might care very little about you.

Remember that a modest and classy look is also attractive—especially to those who value modesty and class. The Book of Mormon records a rare occasion when the Nephites were prosperous *and* righteous at the same time, and it comments on their clothes in these words: "And they did not wear costly apparel, yet they were neat and comely" (Alma 1:27). I looked up "comely" in the dictionary, and do you know what it means? Attractive. So when you dress, you have to ask yourself a question: Whom am I trying to attract? What type of person would be attracted to me if I dress like this? Those who value modesty or those who don't? And if they don't value modesty, how would they feel about my other standards?

There's another thing you must remember about the impact of dressing immodestly. Suppose there's a guy out there who you really admire and respect. Suppose he's doing his best to be a good person and is on track for graduating from high school and serving a mission. And suppose someone comes along who is dressed immodestly. What will he do? He'll probably turn away. Why? Because he's trying to control his thoughts, and the way some girls dress makes thought control difficult. So instead of being *attractive,* the young woman who dresses immodesty is actually *repulsive.* Joy Saunders Lundberg told this story about her nephew:

> When one of my returned-missionary nephews was visiting me one day, I asked him about a girl he had been dating. He said, "Oh, we're not dating any more." Though they hadn't dated long, I had the impression he had been quite interested in her. She had seemed to be a good LDS girl. I asked what happened.
>
> "I was starting to fall for her," he said, "and . . . well . . .

to tell you the truth, she started wearing clothes that were a little too revealing. I don't mean to sound stuffy, but, honestly, I began to feel uncomfortable. Not because she wasn't pretty to look at, but because I didn't like what it made me think about. I've been trying all my life to be morally clean, and . . . well, I just couldn't chance it, so I broke it off" (in *Why Say No When the World Says Yes? Resisting Temptation in an Immoral World*, comp. Randal A. Wright [Salt Lake City: Deseret Book, 1993], 47–48).

The way you dress will either help the Holy Spirit do his work or help the evil spirit do his work. I doubt that any Latter-day Saint young women would want to help Satan do his work.

CLASS OR CRASS?

Recently my bishop was preparing to talk to the young women of my ward about the way they dress. Guess where he went to get some advice? To the young men. And what did they say? They said it was hard for them to be around the girls who dressed immodestly. It made them feel uncomfortable and a little embarrassed. They appreciated the girls who dressed modestly because they were easier to be around. They were easier to talk to and make friends with.

I really wish I could use stronger terms about the influence immodest clothing can have on young men, but I'd rather have a woman do that so that I don't blush. Two women would be even better. I'd now like to introduce Irene Ericksen and Jan Pinborough. They wrote a book for college-age young women called *Where Do I Go from Here?* Their section on modesty was superb. Here it is:

> One of the best ways you can "stand as a witness of God" is in the way you dress. How do you want to be treated by those around you? With respect and dignity? How do you

hope that young men—and eventually your husband—will treat you? Do you want them to see you as a person first, a soul who has feelings and thoughts? Do you want to help them keep their thoughts clean or be a stumbling block to them? The way you choose to dress plays a big role in determining how others—particularly men—perceive and treat you.

Men's sexual responses are more easily triggered by visual stimuli than are women's. Tight clothing that accentuates the shape of a woman's bust or bottom, clothing that is strapless, off-the-shoulder, low-cut, or shows cleavage, or bares her stomach, back, or thigh immediately draws a man's attention to that part of the woman's body. These visual cues usually trigger sexually oriented feelings, which the man may or may not choose to suppress. He will find it difficult *not* to think of the woman as a physical object first, rather than as a human soul.

If this is hard for you to believe, it is probably because this is not how *you* respond to visual stimuli. And, you might think, if you can control your thoughts, why shouldn't men be able to? Simply stated, men are "wired" differently than women. Their reaction is, at least in part, a matter of biology. So when you wear revealing clothing, you are creating a stumbling block for men around you. And this is something the Lord may hold us accountable for as women.

On the other hand, when you dress modestly, you help men think of you as a person first, not as an object of physical desire. This does not mean that you should strive to look unattractive, but rather *to be attractive in a modest way.* Many of the styles for young women today are immodest. Some are *very* immodest. But because standards have changed so much in the last ten years, you may not recognize it. So dressing modestly is a challenge. When you get dressed, take a hard look in the mirror and ask, "Does my clothing cling to my body and accentuate my bust and hips? Does my cleavage show, or can someone see down my shirt when I lean forward? Is more of my thigh showing than is not showing? Is my midriff showing?"

You might also ask, "Does my clothing call attention to my body or my beliefs?" Or to put it another way, "Am I wearing the uniform of a daughter of God or a singer on a music video?" . . . You can also ask for feedback from your mother, a female seminary or institute teacher, or an LDS friend. Above all, pray and ask your Heavenly Father how he wants you to look to others.

As you dress in a way that shows respect for yourself and your male friends, you will help to de-sexualize the atmosphere between women and men. This is good for both women and men. Today, more than ever, the Lord needs young Latter-day Saint women to "stand as a witness" by dressing modestly (*Where Do I Go from Here?* [Salt Lake City: Bookcraft, 2002], 73–75).

Again, you want to be valued for *you*—not for the body you came in. We don't love our grandmas because they look like supermodels. We love them because of who they are. And while we should always take care of ourselves and dress attractively, our real beauty comes from within.

I have a friend named Barbara Barrington Jones who wrote a book titled *The Inside-Outside Beauty Book.* Sister Jones used to train contestants for the Miss USA pageant, and she was quite successful. As part of their training, each contestant had to write five thank-you notes per day. On some days the contestants had a hard time thinking of five people to thank, but Sister Jones made them persist until they wrote the notes anyway.

Why would she make them do that? It had nothing to do with eyeliner, rouge, or base. It had no relation to hips and thighs and high heels. It was completely unrelated to waving, smiling, and balancing a crown. Sister Jones made them write thank-you notes because she knew that a person who is *gracious* is a person who is *beautiful*. Sister Jones, a recognized expert on beauty, knows that real, lasting beauty always comes from within.

THE EYES HAVE IT

Dressing modestly is an issue for boys *and* girls, men *and* women. On page sixteen, *For the Strength of Youth* says, "All should avoid extremes in clothing, appearance, and hairstyle." "All" means every person of every gender. My friend Brad Wilcox once wrote, "We should dress so that the first thing others notice about us is our face" (*Growing Up* [Salt Lake City: Deseret Book, 2000], 47).

Once while speaking at a fireside about standards, I stopped suddenly and said, "Look at me!" Everyone in the congregation did exactly as I asked. They looked at *me*. They looked at my eyes. Can you imagine how strange it would have been if I had said, "Look at me!" and the entire group focused on my right elbow? Or my left hand? Or my knee? Those things aren't *me*. If you want to look at me, you look in my eyes. If I want to look at you, I look in your eyes.

Some girls want boys to notice them, but they dress so that boys' eyes will be drawn somewhere other than their faces. They want the attention, but their bodies get in the way. Similarly, some boys do extreme things to their hair—spiking or bleaching it, cutting it into a Mohawk, or turning it into a huge *fro*. I recently saw a boy at a youth conference with a spherical hair thing so large and so high that it was difficult to notice anything about him but his hair. I can only imagine what would have happened had he walked into a room with a low-hanging ceiling fan. Twist and shout! Once again, something got in the way of his eyes.

Also, some boys like to wear their pants so low that they look like they're going to fall off. It may be fashionable to some, but it's extreme, and it draws attention away from their eyes. Most important, it's not the way a young man who holds the Aaronic Priesthood and has taken upon him the name of Christ should dress.

Kirk Tenney, a teachers quorum adviser from Las Vegas, once asked the young men in his class, "How many of you passed the sacrament last week?" They all raised their hands, to which he responded, "I didn't see any of you pass the sacrament." They replied, "Yes we did." Then Brother Tenney said, "When I turned to reach out to the bread tray, I saw Darth Mall. That's the first thing I saw. When the water came around, I didn't see a teacher, I saw a Tasmanian devil." He was talking about the young men's neckties.

Then Brother Tenney pulled out a sack of his own favorite ties and offered the young men the opportunity to trade for something more appropriate to wear while passing the sacrament. He taught the young men the same principle we discussed above. Members of the Aaronic Priesthood wear white shirts and conservative neckties so that they don't detract from the reverence the sacrament deserves. During the sacrament, we want people to be able to focus on the Savior, not on movie advertisements on our neckties. In the same way, our clothes and fashions should draw others' eyes to our eyes, not to other parts of our bodies.

WHEN FASHION IS A PAIN

In the past few years I've met young people with pierced eyebrows, pierced tongues, and pierced noses. As my eyes have noticed their various facial perforations, a certain word always pops into my mind: *Ow!* I normally have another thought too: *That looks horrible. Why would you do that to yourself?* I won't pretend to understand some fads. I freely admit that I just don't get it. As a general rule, I try to avoid wearing things that cause pain, make people grimace, or set off metal detectors at airports. Some young people dress outrageously to irritate old people, go against the norm, or get attention. If attention is what they want, I suppose they get some. But it's too bad they puncture their faces in the process.

A few years ago while waiting in a doctor's office, I read a magazine article about tattoos and piercings that I found very interesting, and I think you will too:

Piercing: the hole thing

how: A needle or stud makes a hole in the skin. . . .

temporary effects: To heal, a piercing takes a week or two (ears, eyebrow) to a month or more (navel, nose, tongue). Cleanliness is *superimportant.* For a bottom lip piercing, swill Listerine. Eating and speaking are tricky for a few days with a pierced tongue. Watch for redness or itching, which may signal an infection or allergy to nickel (most silver and gold jewelry contains a trace of it for strength).

removal: Piercings are easily abandoned but can leave permanent evidence. Heidi Sherman, an editor at [this magazine] had a bellyful of trouble with her belly button. "The ring leaned a bit and rubbed where my jeans' waist is. I had to be careful what I wore," Sherman says. "It's been out seven years and has left a big brown dot." . . .

Tattoo or not tattoo?

. . . **where:** Dye is injected into the skin's top layers. Needles of varying sizes are dipped in pigment, which is drawn into a tube in the needle. As the needles make holes, color enters the skin. . . .

temporary effects: Getting a tattoo means needles puncturing your skin over and over. It's painful. For a week or two you have to clean the tattoo with an antibacterial agent, slather on antibiotic cream and keep it covered. Pools are out for a while—water and sun can damage the color.

risks: Any cutting of the skin opens you up to hazards that include hepatitis, TB and HIV. Yellow and red dyes can sometimes produce allergic reactions if exposed to the sun.

Sounds pretty negative, doesn't it? So what magazine do you think I got that from? *Parents* magazine? *Discourage Your Teen* magazine? *Limit Freedom Monthly?* No. It was from the June 2000 issue of *Seventeen* ("Body Art," 194–96)—not exactly a conservative publication. I appreciate the honesty in the article, but the Church doesn't look to *Seventeen* for help with rules, principles, and doctrines. We look to the Lord and his servants.

On page sixteen, our current *For the Strength of Youth* warns us of the painful fashions mentioned above in these words: "Do not disfigure yourself with tattoos or body piercings. If girls or women desire to have their ears pierced, they are encouraged to wear only one pair of modest earrings."

Someone may be thinking, "But Brother Bytheway, would wearing one extra set of earrings really keep me out of heaven?" All of my rigorous training and vast experience leads to me to answer, "I don't know." So I'm not much help. Let's ask someone smarter than I am. Elder M. Russell Ballard spoke of a young Laurel who answered that question for herself:

> I know a 17-year-old who, just prior to the prophet's talk, had pierced her ears a second time. She came home from the fireside, took off the second set of earrings, and simply said to her parents, "If President Hinckley says we should only wear one set of earrings, that's good enough for me."
>
> Wearing two pair of earrings may or may not have eternal consequences for this young woman, *but her willingness to obey the prophet will.* . . . Are we listening, brothers and sisters? Are we hearing the words of the prophet to us as parents, as youth leaders, and as youth? Or are we allowing ourselves . . . to be blinded by pride and stubbornness, which could prevent us from receiving the blessings that come from following the teachings of God's prophet? ("'His Word Ye Shall Receive,'" *Ensign,* May 2001, 66; emphasis added).

I love what Elder Ballard said. The earrings may or may not

have eternal consequences, but "her willingness to obey the prophet will." Bingo! That's the point. It's not about your ears; it's about your attitude! It's not about your hemlines; it's about your heart! It's not about your dress; it's about your disposition! What does the Lord require? "Behold the Lord requireth the heart and a willing mind; and the willing and obedient shall eat the good of the land of Zion in these last days" (D&C 64:34).

How do you know if your heart is willing? Look at your wardrobe. But someone may say, "But it's my body, so it's my choice, right?" To answer that question, let's again look at what a prophet has said. (You know we're a little dense when the Apostle Paul has to begin a scripture like this: "What?") Notice below how quickly Paul gets to the doctrine: our body is a place for the Holy Ghost to dwell. Also, notice who your body really belongs to.

> What? Know ye not that your body is the temple of the Holy Ghost which is in you, which ye have of God, and ye are not your own? For ye are bought with a price: therefore glorify God in your body, and in your spirit, which are God's (1 Corinthians 6:19–20).

You and I are "bought with a price." What was the price? It was suffering beyond anything we can imagine by Jesus Christ (D&C 19:16–19). When we take a coupon to the grocery store, we say, "I'd like to redeem this coupon." We then use the coupon to buy something. Jesus bought us with his blood, which is why we call him our Redeemer (Acts 20:28). We are not our own. We belong to him because we have made a covenant to take his name upon us and to keep the commandments he has given us (Mosiah 26:18; 18:10).

READ ALL ABOUT IT

Fortunately, many Latter-day Saint young women are changing the world instead of letting the world change them. And

Latter-day Saints are not the only ones concerned about the fashion trends of increasing immodesty. Let me show you a sampling of newspaper stories from around the country:

Fashion, Not Flashin'

**Surf City Teen Kristi Wilson Proudly Strutted
Her Modest Wear in a Fashion Show at Nordstrom
on Saturday**

"I cannot describe the feeling [of] . . . being able to get up there in front of all my friends modeling clothing I felt completely comfortable in," Wilson said. "It has always been so hard to find tops that aren't too short or pants that aren't too low, [and] finding prom dresses was the biggest nightmare."

As a Mormon teen, her standards for clothing are more conservative than the standards reflected in much of the clothing offered today by a Britney Spears-Christina Aguilera-J. Lo-influenced fashion industry (Michele Marr, *Huntington Beach Independent,* 3 April 2003, A-7).

Modest Dream

Finding the Perfect Prom Dress—with Sleeves

In a world where teen fashion seems all about showing something—a midriff, a shoulder, a cheeky bra strap, even—there are about 4,800 girls in Arizona shopping for prom dresses with one caveat: They can't, and some don't want to, show anything at all.

Mostly, they are Mormons, members of The Church of Jesus Christ of Latter-day Saints, but are joined by other conservative or religious girls, and by a few peers who've tired of the Britney Spears look (Jaimee Rose, *The Arizona Republic,* 26 April 2003, E-1)

A Modest Proposal

Mormon Girls Line Up for Fashion Show Featuring Less Skin

Thanks to the unlikely collaboration of two fashion-frustrated Mormon moms and customer-friendly Nordstrom, [Anaheim High School senior Katie Sereno] has an alternative—more than 30 of them. A Nordstrom in Costa Mesa was hosting a sold-out fashion show this weekend featuring 33 Mormon teenage girls from Southern California wearing stylish dresses with not a spaghetti strap in sight (William Lobdell, *San Francisco Chronicle,* 12 October 2002, A-2).

Parents Refuse to Buy Risqué Outfits for Girls

A growing number of parents are becoming outraged by the proliferation of provocative clothes for their children, particularly in the preteen departments. As they take their daughters back-to-school shopping, they say they won't buckle under societal pressures to transform their teens into clones of Britney Spears or Christina Aguilera (*The Washington Times,* 9 August 2001).

Yes indeed. Latter-day Saint teenagers don't have to go with the flow of the world. They can go against the grain, make some noise, and change some hearts. Here are some websites for finding modest prom dresses: modestbydesign.com, modestprom.com, greatlengths.com, latterdaybride.com.

BEFORE I CLOTHES

If we had a top-five chart of reasons to dress modestly and avoid extremes, what would the list look like? It might include these items:

1. What you wear sends a message about who you are and what you believe. You're a high-class person, a son or

daughter of God who has taken upon yourself the name of
Christ, so make your clothes match your message.

2. If you hope to be *attractive by dressing immodestly, you*
may actually be *repulsive* to the very people you're hoping
to attract.
3. Real beauty comes from within—always has, always will.
4. If people aren't looking at our eyes because of the way we
dress, they're seeing our body as an object, and they're not
seeing the real us.
5. Our body is not really ours. It has been bought with a price
and is a temple for the Holy Ghost.

We've talked about rules and we've mentioned a few principles, but once again, we've noticed the doctrine behind the
standards. The guidelines are all intended to help us keep the
Spirit—the gift of the Holy Ghost. President Harold B. Lee
taught:

> Do not underestimate the important symbolic and actual
> effect of appearance. Persons who are well groomed and
> modestly dressed invite the companionship of the Spirit of
> our Father in Heaven and are able to exercise a wholesome
> influence upon those around them. Persons who are unkempt
> and careless about their appearance, or adopt the visual sym-
> bols of those who often oppose our ideals, expose them-
> selves and persons around them to influences that are
> degrading and dissonant. Outward appearance is often a
> reflection of inward tendencies (*The Teachings of Harold B.
> Lee,* ed. Clyde J. Williams [Salt Lake City: Bookcraft, 1996],
> 220).

Thanks for reading. That was a tough chapter to write. I hope
it was convincing without being annoying. Another tough chapter
is next.

DATING

6. You are about to turn sixteen. What is the dating standard outlined by the First Presidency?

    A. Date only Church members, go on group or double dates, and don't date before you're sixteen.

    B. Date only those who have high standards and in whose company you can maintain your standards, and don't date before you're sixteen.

    C. Sit down with your parents and set your own standards.

    D. There are no specific guidelines other than to "choose wisely" and "bridle your passions."

    E. Set standards based on popular TV shows named after zip codes.

The correct answer is B.

Most teenagers never turn fifteen years old. They just skip that year. They're either fourteen or "almost sixteen." Sixteen is an age to look forward to because of the two D's: dating and driving. You might be interested to know that your parents think of two corresponding D's when you turn sixteen: depression and dents.

Depression because you're growing up too fast and "dents" because of what happened to the van as a result of the lesson you missed in driver's ed.

Driving is a privilege. And whenever you have a privilege, you also have a responsibility. If you drive irresponsibly by running red lights and rolling through stop signs, you'll lose your privilege to drive. Similarly, the gospel gives us rules in dating, and with the privilege of dating comes responsibility. What responsibility? To pick up the right fork when the salad comes? To let the young man open the car door? No. I believe the Lord is far less concerned about what fork you use than he is about your honor and your virtue. Here's your responsibility:

> A young man and a young woman on a date are responsible to help each other maintain their standards and to protect each other's honor and virtue. You must honor the sanctity of the priesthood and of womanhood (*For the Strength of Youth,* 24).

In driver's education, you learn to stop at stop signs and red lights, signal before turning, and check your blind spot before changing lanes. Do these rules limit your freedom? No, they protect you from consequences. All you have to do is watch one episode of *World's Scariest Police Chases* to see the consequences of driving like an idiot.

BEHIND THE WHEEL OF LIFE

Why have state governments across the country chosen sixteen years old as the age for driving? To be honest, I don't know. Maybe they think you're tall enough by then that you can see the rearview mirror when you sit in the driver's seat. Maybe they figure that at sixteen you've reached a level of trustworthiness and responsibility. Maybe they just had to draw the line somewhere, and they drew it at sixteen.

You may also be wondering, "Why did Church leaders pick the age of sixteen as the age when you can go on dates?" If we read "the rule," we'll find out:

> Do not date until you are at least 16 years old. Dating before then can lead to immorality, limit the number of other young people you meet, and deprive you of experiences that will help you choose an eternal partner (*For the Strength of Youth*, 24).

Perhaps some of the early members of the Church asked why they couldn't use tobacco or alcohol. Back then, the only reason they had for avoiding tobacco was that the prophet asked them to. Today all sorts of medical evidence verifies the Word of Wisdom, but the real reason we obey is because we love the Lord and we've promised to keep his commandments.

To the best of my knowledge, the first time the age of sixteen was mentioned as the age for dating was in the 1965 version of *For the Strength of Youth*. Twenty-three years later, in 1988, someone did a study about what happens to girls who begin dating earlier than sixteen. The results were eye-opening. Ninety-one percent of the girls who began dating at age twelve had had sexual relations by the time they graduated from high school—91 percent! The numbers dropped all the way to 20 percent for those who waited until they were sixteen to begin dating ("Primroses on a Cobblestone Wall," *Church News*, 10 September 1988, 16).

Is this why we don't begin dating until we're sixteen? Because of a chart? No. We wait because of a prophet. But the chart suggests that perhaps President Kimball saw something that others didn't see. Perhaps the Lord inspired President Kimball about the age for dating, as he did about many other things. President Kimball loved the teenagers of the Church, and he wanted them to be protected from the possible consequences of dating too soon. When it comes to driving, waiting until you're sixteen is a law

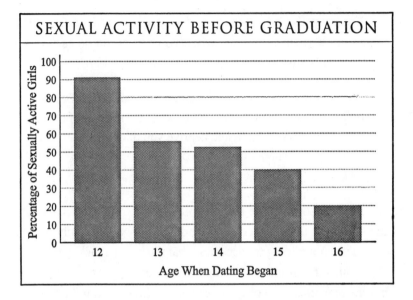

based on your *physical* maturity. When it comes to dating, being willing to wait until you're sixteen will reveal your *spiritual* maturity.

BUT WHAT IS A DATE?

Duh. It's like a big fat raisin with a pit inside. Yes, that's a date too, but what is a *date,* as in, "Do not date until you are at least 16 years old"? We'd better answer that question because I know teenagers who go over to their "friend's" house (a friend who happens to be a member of the opposite sex), sit alone with their friend in the basement and watch movies, and sometimes even make out. And then they say they're not dating: "Well, he didn't come and pick me up in a car, so it's not a date."

Oh, spare me. Come on, chosen generation. We have to be wiser than a cup of lint. If a date is only a date when someone picks you up in a car, then people have broken the law of chastity who've never been on a date.

If you arrange to spend time with a member of the opposite sex, and you like each other, I'd say that's a date. "But what about group dates?" Obviously a "group date" is a date, and you've been asked to wait until you're sixteen for those types of dates too. Unfortunately some dates that begin as a "group" end up with a group of pairs. You'll often hear adults use the phrase "paired off" or "pairing off." When you go "off" in "pairs," that's a dating situation, and deep down, every honest teenager knows it. When you're away from the group and alone in pairs, it's easier to be tempted and to get into trouble. The counsel from the First Presidency sums it up nicely.

> "When you begin dating, go in groups or on double dates. Avoid going on frequent dates with the same person. Make sure your parents meet those you date. You may want to invite your dates to activities with your family. Plan dating activities that are positive and inexpensive and that will help you get to know each other. Do things that will help you and your companions maintain your self-respect and remain close to the Spirit of the Lord (*For the Strength of Youth*, 25).

Did you notice that the last words in the dating standard reveal the doctrine behind all the rules? "Remain close to the Spirit of the Lord." Your Heavenly Father loves you, and he asks you to be wise. With the privilege of dating comes the responsibility of keeping the Spirit with you.

BUT THE DANCE IS JUST BARELY BEFORE MY BIRTHDAY!

Someday you'll be a youth leader in your own ward. You might also be a parent. Mark my words, a fifteen-year-old will ask this very question: "But I'm almost sixteen, so isn't it okay?" And that same teenager may ask another question: "Well, did *you* date before *you* were sixteen?" All the teenagers in the ward will be on the edge of their folding chairs waiting for your response. What will you say?

Most schools have dances. Some are informal, where you can go alone or with a group of friends. Other school dances, like the junior prom or girl's choice, are for couples, so everyone is expected to bring a date. Let's say there are fifteen come-with-a-date dances during your sophomore, junior, and senior years and that you'll be old enough to attend thirteen of those dances. When you look back on your life, will it really make a huge difference that you went to thirteen dances instead of fifteen? The fact is, by the time you're a youth leader you'll have a hard time remembering how many school dances you attended. But you will remember that you waited until you were sixteen. That knowledge will give you peace in your heart for years to come, and it will help you answer future teenagers' questions without blushing or making excuses.

"Brother Bytheway, you just don't get it! If I don't go to this dance, I'll just die! It will be the end of the world!" Yes, of course, the cemeteries are full of girls who "just died" because they didn't go to a dance. It's been the leading cause of teenager deaths for years. And as we can all see, the world ended the first time someone missed a prom back in 1953 and has been ending just about every month since.

Do I sound insensitive? I guess I do. My daughters won't be teenagers for quite a while yet, but I watched my sisters as teenagers. All of them missed dances, and none of them died. And the world didn't end either. To be honest, I sat home during most "girl's choice" dances at my school, and somehow I managed to survive too. (They should call those "Girl's Choice and Accountability" dances. Ha ha.)

I believe the Lord is asking you to be wise and mature beyond your years. (One of the reasons I love the Church is that it expects so much of us.) When your school is having a dance and you're not sixteen, you have a real chance to show the Lord that all those quotes about a "chosen generation" and "saved for the last days" are true. The Lord is asking you to hear the words of the prophet, even if you don't see the reasons clearly right now.

I'm so proud of you for reading this far, and I have great faith that you will make the right decision. The instant you make it, you will feel a sense of satisfaction inside. Your spirit will be lifted, and you might even sense that your Father in Heaven is pleased as well. There's no better feeling in the world.

THE PHONE'S FOR YOU, IT'S . . .

We've talked about when to date, but another important question is whom to date. That's another critical question because nobody ever married anyone they didn't date first (except on mindless Hollywood "reality" shows). Consider this excellent counsel: "Date only those who have high standards and in whose company you can maintain your standards" (*For the Strength of Youth*, 24). Some people have a good influence on you, and some don't. We all know that's true.

Some young people think, "Well, maybe I can help this person," which is a noble thought. But sometimes young people aren't as strong as they think. Instead of lifting another, they find themselves being pulled down. Family and friends may see it happening, but some young people are blind to things happening right before their eyes. When parents say, "I'm worried that he is having a bad influence on you," they respond, "But he's my friend!" As if the word "friend" is some kind of magic disinfectant that erases every bad influence and makes anything the "friend" does okay.

The single best and most useful definition of a friend I've ever heard came from Elder Robert D. Hales, delivered while he was the presiding bishop. He said, "A true friend makes it easier for us to live the gospel" ("The Aaronic Priesthood: Return with Honor," *Ensign*, May 1990, 40). That definition is wonderful. It's concise, it's clear, and it's almost mathematical in its precision. For example, you could write it as an equation:

_____ = makes it easier to live the gospel of Jesus Christ.

You can stick other words in the blank and see if they fit. Try these words and phrases:

- The Book of Mormon = makes it easier to live the gospel of Jesus Christ.
- Seminary = makes it easier to live the gospel of Jesus Christ.
- My Church leaders = make it easier to live the gospel of Jesus Christ.

See? All of those are friends. Do you want to try some tougher ones?

- The clothes I wear = make it easier to live the gospel of Jesus Christ.
- Tonight's episode of *Friends* = makes it easier to live the gospel of Jesus Christ.
- The Austin Powers movie we rented = makes it easier to live the gospel of Jesus Christ.
- The music I listen to = makes it easier to live the gospel of Jesus Christ.
- The person I'm dating = makes it easier to live the gospel of Jesus Christ.

You see how well that works? If the person you're dating, the entertainment you choose, and the clothes you wear don't make it easier to live the gospel, then you're flirting with the enemy. You're pushing away the Holy Ghost and inviting another spirit to influence your life. It's nothing to laugh at either. Here's what that enemy is all about:

> He is working under such perfect disguise that many do not recognize either him or his methods. There is no crime he would not commit, no debauchery he would not set up, no plague he would not send, no heart he would not break, no life he would not take, no soul he would not destroy. He comes as a thief in the night; he is a wolf in sheep's clothing

(*Messages of the First Presidency,* comp. James R. Clark, 6 vols. [Salt Lake City: Bookcraft, 1965–75], 6:179).

Yes, Satan works under "perfect disguise," and one of the reasons we strive to keep the Holy Ghost with us is so that we can see things we normally wouldn't see.

The greatest blessing I had in high school was not being captain of the football team (I wasn't). It was not being tall, dark, and handsome (0 for three). It was not having a nice car (I usually drove my Dad's 1964 Dodge Polara). My greatest blessing, which my parents also commented on from time to time, was that I had good friends—friends who had high standards and who never asked me to compromise those standards. They were friends who made it easier for me to live the gospel.

If I said, "Mom, Dad, I'm going somewhere with my friends," which I did many times a week, they'd say, "Have fun!" because they knew my friends were real friends in the best definition of the word. If it's important to have friends who make living the gospel easier, it's even more important of those we choose to date. So whom do you date? You date those who help you maintain your standards. In other words, you date true friends.

MORALITY

7. You are old enough to date. What are the standards about physical affection outlined by the First Presidency?

A. Always treat your date with respect.

B. Stay in areas of safety where you can easily control your physical feelings.

C. Do not participate in talk or activities that arouse sexual feelings.

D. Do not participate in passionate kissing, lie on top of another person, or touch the private, sacred parts of another person's body, with or without clothing.

E. All of the above.

The answer is E: All of the above.

WHEN, WHO, AND WHAT

We've talked about when you can start dating and a little about whom to date, but we haven't talked about what to do on dates. There are millions of dating ideas out there—all kinds of fun activities that will enable you to get to know other people and have fun. The focus of this book is standards, so I won't go into a list of dating ideas here.

One of the choices you'll have to make concerns your behavior toward others of the opposite sex. The decisions you make in this area will have an impact on your reputation, your happiness, and even your eternal life, so you'd better think them through and choose wisely. Remember this: "Not all teenagers need to date or even want to. Many young people do not date during their teen years because they are not yet interested, do not have opportunities, or simply want to delay forming serious relationships" (*For the Strength of Youth,* 24).

In other words, you have no obligation to date. It's not a contest. It's not a requirement for graduation. If you're eighteen, and you've never been on a date, no big deal. You won't be arrested by the dating police. I think most fathers out there would be delighted if their children didn't date until they were seventeen or eighteen. Along with dating come many pressures and choices, which some teenagers are simply not ready to handle.

Part of what makes dating so potentially dangerous is what can happen when two people, teenagers or adults, are out alone. We all have desires and urges that the Lord has asked us, even commanded us, to control. One of the most common teenage questions at a standards night is, "How far is too far?" The question always makes me a little uncomfortable because it seems to focus on "how close can I get to the forbidden area" instead of on "how close can I stay to the safe area." But if you want the answer, it is available.

A number of years ago at general priesthood meeting, Elder Richard G. Scott addressed some of these tough issues in a question-and-answer format:

> **Question:** They always tell us we shouldn't become sexually involved, but they never tell us the limits. What are they?

Answer: Any sexual intimacy outside of the bonds of marriage—I mean any intentional contact with the sacred, private parts of another's body, with or without clothing—is a sin and is forbidden by God. It is also a transgression to intentionally stimulate these emotions within your own body. Satan tempts one to believe that there are allowable levels of physical contact between consenting individuals who seek the powerful stimulation of emotions they produce, and if kept within bounds, no harm will result. As a witness of Jesus Christ, I testify that is absolutely false ("Making the Right Choices," *Ensign,* November 1994, 38).

You'll notice that the newest *For the Strength of Youth* uses some of the exact phrases from Elder Scott's talk:

Do not do anything to arouse the powerful emotions that must be expressed only in marriage. Do not participate in passionate kissing, lie on top of another person, or touch the private, sacred parts of another person's body, with or without clothing. Do not allow anyone to do that with you. Do not arouse those emotions in your own body (*For the Strength of Youth,* 27).

So there it is. Very nicely and specifically spelled out. You may want to read it over a few times to make sure you understand. You'll notice that neither Elder Scott nor the *For the Strength of Youth* pamphlet used the phrase "of the opposite sex." The behavior described is forbidden by God regardless of the gender of the two people involved.

KISSES—WORTH WAITING FOR OR WORTHLESS?

The standard mentions "passionate kissing" as a line you must not approach. Just remember that you will be much more respected for what you withhold than for what you give out. Just as you have no obligation to date, you also have no obligation to express affection. At this time in your life your dating should be for fun and to get to know others. No one who takes you out on a date should expect any kind of physical affection in return, and you are under no obligation to give any. You'll be more respected if you're very careful about how you give out affection.

Many years ago a young man named Alvin W. Jones III gave me a poem he wrote about kissing.

The more the dollar is printed, the less each one is worth.
And so it is with kisses you've given since your birth.
The value of your kisses, a sample cannot measure,
Nor is your kiss more worthy if it's said to give one pleasure.
The more and more you give away, the better your kiss is
*   known.*
And to all the world, your kiss is cheap, and your affection
*   shown.*
But if you save your kisses, no matter what the cost,
You'll find as time moves forward, a chance you've saved, not
*   lost!*
Then when you find the one you love, with whom you'll live
*   life through,*
Think of the worth of a perfect kiss, if saved for only you.

How much are your kisses worth? One dollar? Two? Do you give them out like free samples at Sam's Club? If you do, what are they worth? About as much as a free sample, right? My friend Rand H. Packer told a story about a girl named Mickie who knew that her kisses were worth more than $122.23.

A guy named Bill . . . had a date with a girl named Mickie, and when she refused to give him a good-night kiss, he said, "Look, Mickie. Ordinarily I can understand being refused a good-night kiss on the first date, but this was the junior prom! The ticket cost me twenty dollars, and the flowers were twelve dollars and ten cents."

She wasn't impressed, so he continued. "The tux rental was thirty bucks, and the spot-remover cost me two dollars and ten cents."

Mickie only looked at him a little sorrowfully, and so he babbled on.

"The taxi ride to dinner was eight dollars and three cents, and the dinner was thirty-five dollars and eighty-three cents!"

Not getting the response he wanted, Bill began to scream. "Refreshments were four dollars and eighty-five cents, and the taxi home was nine dollars and thirty-two cents!"

"So," Mickie asked coolly, "what's your point?"

"Well," Bill said plaintively, "Don'tcha think I deserve just a little something?"

So she wrote him out a check for one hundred twenty-two dollars and twenty-three cents (in *Why Say No When the World Says Yes? Resisting Temptation in an Immoral World,* " comp. Randal A. Wright [Salt Lake City: Deseret Book, 1993], 15–16).

I'm impressed with Mickie because her kisses were not for sale. Unfortunately, some young people become so free with their affection that they ruin their reputations and they lose their self-respect. I am suggesting that you be fairly conservative. And don't ever feel embarrassed if you've never kissed anyone. That time will come. For now, you can just tell people, "My kisses are so wonderful and incredible that I just don't give them out. You've no idea the stir it would cause all over the world."

THE LINE STARTS IN YOUR HEAD

When teenagers ask adults to define the line ("line hunting," I call it), I'm always reminded of a story I heard as a child. A lumber company was looking for someone to haul logs out of a steep canyon. Three applicants interviewed for the job. "How good of a driver are you?" the interviewer asked. "I'm so good," said the first applicant, "that I can keep my tires only a foot away from the edge of the road and not go over the side." The second applicant had a similar response. "I'm such a skilled driver," he said, "that I can keep my wheels only six inches away and never go off the edge." When the third applicant was asked the same question, he replied, "I'm a very good driver that you can trust. I stay as far away from the edge as I can." Obviously, the third applicant was hired. Seeing how close we can get to the edge is a foolish and dangerous strategy, both in driving and in dating.

One of the reasons it's so difficult to define "the line" is that we can also cross a line in our thoughts. When Jesus delivered the Sermon on the Mount, he gave what we often call the "higher law." He said, "Ye have heard that it was said by them of old time, Thou shalt not kill . . . but I say unto you, that whosoever is angry with his brother without a cause shall be in danger of the judgment" (Matthew 5:21–22).

Jesus "raised the bar," so to speak. Not only should we not kill but also we should not be angry with our brother! Jesus continued, "Ye have heard that it was said by them of old time, Thou shalt not commit adultery: But I say unto you, that whosoever looketh on a woman to lust after her hath committed adultery with her already in his heart" (Matthew 5:27–28). Jesus condemned adultery as well as lusting in one's heart. So the law of chastity isn't only about our outward actions—the physical line. It's also about our thoughts and inner desires! President Spencer W. Kimball taught:

> Thoughts largely determine immorality of acts. Holding hands would generally not be immoral, but it would depend on whether or not one's mind ran rampant. An embrace may not be immoral, but if the closeness of the body awakens immoral desires, then that is another thing. . . . One must

keep the thoughts clean. . . . Two people could embrace, kiss, dance, look, and I can conceive of one of them being immoral and the other innocent of sin (*The Teachings of Spencer W. Kimball,* ed. Edward L. Kimball [Salt Lake City: Bookcraft 1982], 282).

Do you remember Corianton from your scripture study? He was one of the sons of Alma the Younger who broke the law of chastity while he should have been doing missionary work. What led Corianton to break the law of chastity? The Book of Mormon teaches us that it started in his inner desires and thoughts. When Alma talked to his son, he didn't immediately chastise him for breaking the law of chastity. He began by pointing out where the sin began.

1. "Thou didst go on unto boasting in thy strength and thy wisdom" (Alma 39:2). In modern language, we'd say, "You said to yourself, 'I can handle it. I attended all those standards nights and read all those standards pamphlets, but I know what I'm doing. I'm in control.'"

2. "Thou didst forsake the ministry" (Alma 39:3). Modern language: "You weren't where you were supposed to be! If you're trying to get over alcoholism, you probably shouldn't hang out in a bar. If you can't swim, you shouldn't go out in the ocean in a leaky canoe. You were supposed to stand in holy places."

3. "Thou didst . . . go . . . after the harlot Isabel" (Alma 39:3). Modern language: "You were with the wrong crowd (to put it mildly). You were with friends who did not respect your standards and would not help you maintain your standards."

The sin began in Corianton's head and heart. The great lesson in all of this is that none of us can be so prideful as to think, "Hey, I can handle it." The fact is, if any of us, old or young, allow ourselves to think that we can "handle it" and find ourselves with the wrong crowd rather than where we are supposed to be, we could fall. President Gordon B. Hinckley taught:

> I am reminded of what I heard from a man—a great, strong, and wise man—who served in the presidency of this Church years ago. His daughter was going out on a date, and her father said to her, "Be careful. Be careful of how you act and what you say."
>
> She replied, "Daddy, don't you trust me?" He responded, "I don't entirely trust myself. One never gets too old nor too high in the Church that the adversary gives up on him" ("Trust and Accountability," *Brigham Young University 1992–93 Devotional and Fireside Speeches* [Provo, Utah: University Publications, 1993], 24).

President Hinckley has confidence in you and in your ability to see right from wrong. He knows that deep down you know where the lines are.

> My dear young friends, in matters of sex you know what is right. You know when you are walking on dangerous ground, when it is so easy to stumble and slide into the pit of transgression. I plead with you to be careful, to stand safely back from the cliff of sin over which it is so easy to fall. Keep yourselves clean from the dark and disappointing evil of sexual transgression. Walk in the sunlight of that peace which comes from obedience to the commandments of the Lord ("A Prophet's Counsel and Prayer for Youth," *Ensign,* January 2001, 8).

You'll notice that President Hinckley didn't describe a line on a flat surface but rather as a "cliff of sin." That's why "line hunting" can be so dangerous. One minute you're on safe ground, and the next minute you're falling. A number of years ago, I got stuck in the Ontario, California, airport. I decided to use my layover

time to memorize a poem. (As you read, think about the "cliff of
sin" that President Hinckley mentioned.)

A Fence or an Ambulance

'Twas a dangerous cliff, as they freely confessed,
Though to walk near its crest was so pleasant;
But over its terrible edge there had slipped
A duke and full many a peasant.
So the people said something would have to be done,
But their project did not at all tally;
Some said, "Put a fence around the edge of the cliff,"
Some, "An ambulance down in the valley. . . .

"For the cliff is all right, if you're careful," they said,
And, if folks even slip and are dropping,
It isn't the slipping that hurts them so much,
As the shock down below when they're stopping."
So day after day, as these mishaps occurred,
Quick forth would these rescuers sally
To pick up the victims who fell off the cliff,
With their ambulance down in the valley.

Then an old sage remarked: "It's a marvel to me
That people give far more attention
To repairing results than to stopping the cause,
When they'd much better aim at prevention.
Let us stop at its source all this mischief," cried he,
"Come, neighbors and friends, let us rally;
If the cliff we will fence we might almost dispense
With the ambulance down in the valley."

"Oh, he's a fanatic," the others rejoined,
"Dispense with the ambulance? Never!
He'd dispense with all charities, too, if he could;
No! No! We'll support them forever.
Aren't we picking up folks just as fast as they fall?

And shall this man dictate to us? Shall he?
Why should people of sense stop to put up a fence,
While the ambulance works in the valley?" . . .
Better guide well the young than reclaim them when old,
For the voice of true wisdom is calling,
"To rescue the fallen is good, but 'tis best
To prevent other people from falling."
Better close up the source of temptation and crime
Than deliver from dungeon or galley;
Better put a strong fence round the top of the cliff
Than an ambulance down in the valley.

> (Joseph Malins, in *Best Loved Poems of the LDS People* [Salt Lake City: Deseret Book, 1996], 302–4).

So what is the ambulance? It's repentance. What is the fence? It's the standards that were put in place not to limit freedom but to protect from consequences. I think an ambulance is a good representation of repentance. Repentance is not easy, and it hurts. All of us need repentance to one degree or another, so we're all glad the ambulance is there. Cecil B. DeMille, who produced such classic movies as *The Ten Commandments* and *Ben Hur,* once said, "Men and nations cannot really break the Ten Commandments; they can only break themselves against them" (Ezra Taft Benson, "America at the Crossroads," *New Era,* July 1978, 38).

Obviously it would be better to stay within the fence than to break ourselves against the commandments and go for an ambulance ride. President Ezra Taft Benson said it this way, "When it comes to the law of chastity, it is better to prepare and prevent than it is to repair and repent" (Ezra Taft Benson, *The Teachings of Ezra Taft Benson* [Salt Lake City: Bookcraft, 1988], 285).

Which should we talk more about? How bad it is to sin or how to repent? That's an excellent question. We should all be warned about the dangers of sin, but we must also know how to repent. Notice how President Harold B. Lee felt about this question:

> Beware of the awfulness of sin. The more I see of life, the more I am convinced that we must impress you young people with the awfulness of sin rather than to content ourselves with merely teaching the way of repentance. I wish that someone could warn you of the night of hell that follows the committing of a moral sin or of a beastly act (*The Teachings of Harold B. Lee,* ed. Clyde J. Williams [Salt Lake City: Bookcraft, 1996], 225).

Every choice you make has a consequence. Some consequences are brief, and some consequences are long. Throughout this book I have argued that the doctrine behind each of the standards involves keeping the Holy Ghost with you. The consequences of breaking the law of chastity are misery, regret, guilt, and loss of the Spirit. The consequences of keeping the law of chastity and of waiting until after marriage to use your powers to bring children into the world are peace, joy, and happiness. My friend Randal A. Wright has written:

> One day while I was sitting at my desk at the LDS institute where I served as director, a former student named Veronica suddenly burst into my office. She was literally jumping up and down with excitement. I couldn't imagine what all the commotion was about. I thought maybe she had won the Publisher's Clearing House million-dollar prize or something. When she finally calmed down enough to speak, she blurted out her news. "I'm pregnant!" she exclaimed. Her excitement was greater than that of most newly expectant mothers because for many years doctors had doubted her ability even to conceive. And now she was pregnant. All of us who knew her were ecstatic over this news.
>
> What a contrast this visit was to another I received. The

institute secretary knocked on my door and said a young woman wanted to talk to me. I could tell something was seriously wrong as soon as Maria walked through the door. Concern was written all over her face. When I asked how she was doing, she burst into tears. I had no idea what was wrong and had to wait until she got control of her emotions to find out. At first I thought maybe a loved one had died or that she had some incurable disease. It wasn't either of these things. When she finally managed to compose herself, she announced somberly, "I'm pregnant" (in *Why Say No When the World Says Yes? Resisting Temptation in an Immoral World*, 52–53).

Brother Wright went on to explain that both girls had used the same phrase, "I'm pregnant." The difference was in the *timing*. The first girl was married; the second was not. For one, it was an incredibly happy time; for the other, a time of regret, shame, and sorrow. When we don't follow the Lord's standards, or when we refuse to listen to the Lord when he says, "No!" or "Not yet!" we open ourselves up to some sobering consequences.

Some young people think that the standards are a pain. Well, if you want to look at them that way, you can. Just remember the old saying, "There are two kinds of pain in life; the pain of discipline, and the pain of regret. Discipline weighs ounces, but regret weighs tons." I'll take an ounce of discipline over a ton of regret anytime.

When it comes to dating, I'm reminded of what my friend Michael Wilcox often asks his institute students. "Where are you going? Who are you going with?" You may feel as if you hear those questions every night from your parents, but read them again. Where are you going? (Hint: you want to go to the happiest place in the universe—the celestial kingdom). If that's where you really want to go, you can't get there alone. So the next question becomes even more important. "Who are you going with?" Does that person share your standards and goals? Does that person also want, more than anything, to go with you to the celestial kingdom? If not, then where you're going is somewhere else.

Dating and morality are critical topics because they have so much impact on your future happiness. Be tough, be strong, and be careful. You've never heard anyone say, "I'm a happier person because I broke the law of chastity." Or, "I'm a happier person because I started dating too soon." Some things are simply worth waiting for. And don't forget—someone is out there waiting for you.

ACE IT
AND BE HAPPY

A farmer once observed that whenever he put his cows in an enclosed area to graze, a few always pushed against the fence. Within the fenced area were acres of lush, green grass, but some cows seemed to ignore what they could have for free, desiring something forbidden instead. While other cows munched and grazed, some would look beyond the boundaries and spend their entire day pushing their heads against the fence.

This book has focused on some of the "don'ts" in gospel living, and there's some danger in that. Unfortunately, some people see the Church as nothing more than a list of things you can't do, but they forget there are "wide open acres of grass" within. The list of interesting, exciting, and wholesome things you can do with your time would be too large to fit in a book.

One of the things I hope you noticed (which I deliberately repeated over and over again in every chapter) was that the standards are intended to help you keep the Holy Ghost in your life. But the Spirit's purpose isn't only to defend and protect you against temptation and evil. That's just part of it. People who have the Holy Ghost are happier. It's a fact. The happiest people I've

83

ever met in my life are spiritual people. They have the Spirit of the Lord in their lives, and they enjoy living. You already know this.

Think about the happiest people you know—people in your ward that you love to be around or people that make you want to be a better person. I'll bet you'll notice the same thing. They are spiritual people with the Holy Ghost in their lives.

Don't get the impression that religious people just sit around drawing lines and then worrying that someone will cross them. That's a boring existence. There's more to life, and there's more to the gospel. Heber C. Kimball once said, "I am perfectly satisfied that my Father and my God is a cheerful, pleasant, lively, and good-natured Being. Why? Because I am cheerful, pleasant, lively, and good-natured when I have His Spirit" (in *Journal of Discourses,* 26 vols. [London: Latter-day Saints' Book Depot, 1854–86], 4:222.)

People with the Holy Ghost know exactly what they believe, but they also enjoy themselves! The prophet Joseph Smith observed, "The nearer man approaches perfection, the clearer are his views, and the greater his enjoyments, till he has overcome the evils of his life and lost every desire for sin" (Joseph Smith, *Teachings of the Prophet Joseph Smith,* sel. Joseph Fielding Smith [Salt Lake City: Deseret Book, 1976], 51).

The only reason that Church leaders have to keep pointing out the lines is that some members keep flirting with them. (Sometime when you're bored, notice the difference between what Alma says to those in Zarahemla in Alma 5 and what he says to those in Gideon in Alma 7.) Who knows what wonderful things we could hear in general conference if half the talks didn't center on the dangers of pushing against the fence.

Perhaps the prophets would rather focus on more wonderful things, but their job is to warn us of dangers we sometimes don't see. I've often heard teenagers say things like, "I don't see what's wrong with this music," or "I don't see what's wrong with dating before I'm sixteen," or "I don't see the problem with this movie." In every case, they're exactly right. They "don't see."

Fortunately, modern prophets help us to see. The scriptures often compare prophets to "watchmen on the towers" who are able to see danger coming from a long way off. Every general conference we have the opportunity to sustain the First Presidency and the Quorum of the Twelve Apostles as prophets, *seers,* and revelators. What is a seer? It's one who *sees.* It's a *see-er.* While our prophets are doing the work of seeing, Satan does his work of blinding. The Lord told Moses, "And he became Satan, yea, even the devil, the father of all lies, to deceive and to blind men, and to lead them captive at his will, even as many as would not hearken unto my voice" (Moses 4:4; see also S. Michael Wilcox, *Don't Leap with the Sheep* [Salt Lake City: Deseret Book, 2001], 58).

Satan's purpose is to make us miserable (2 Nephi 2:27), while the Lord's purpose is to give us immortality and eternal life (Moses 1:39). Who should we follow? Do the math. This is not a hard decision. The standards of the gospel have blessed my life more than I ever could have imagined.

VICTORY

Several years ago while working for Especially for Youth, I walked into a place called the Garden Court at Brigham Young University. Behind some tables where the box lunches were distributed, I noticed one of the youth counselors. She was tall and slender with long dark hair and gorgeous dark eyes. I watched her for a minute as she was smiling and talking with others, and I was completely smitten. I had met her before and even talked to her, but I think I made my decision at that point. I wanted to ask her out. So I asked her for her phone number and gave her a call. To my surprise (and perhaps because of a recent Relief Society lesson on service to the less fortunate), she said, "Yes."

We went out on our first date one August night, and as I drove home I thought to myself, "She's the one I want." She was funny, she was thoughtful, and she was smart. She beat me on the ACT test, and she had a brown belt in tae kwon do. She was a happy, delightful person who loved the gospel. Of all the girls I had ever gone out with, she was the one I wanted the most. In my day planner I had written the names of several other girls I wanted to go out with, but after that date I crossed out all the other names and underlined her name, "Kim." The only problem was that I had to get her to want me back.

One night, several dates later, we were sitting on her front lawn while I played the guitar and tried to be charming. After we finally got her little brother to leave, I took a deep breath and told her I wasn't interested in dating anyone else but her. She paused, looked at the grass, and finally said, "I have to tell you something."

"Oh boy," I thought, "here it comes." I was expecting something like, "Well, I've been writing to this missionary," or "I think you're a really good friend, but . . ." That's not what she said at all. She said something like, "I think I feel the same way too."

I was so shocked I about broke the guitar in two. As I drove home that night, I had a grin on my face. I kept thinking to myself, "Does that mean I have a girlfriend? Nah, that couldn't be. But if she doesn't want to date anyone else . . . and I don't . . . yeah, that's a girlfriend!" I couldn't stop smiling for the next several days, and we continued to date. Finally, after many more dates, I made arrangements to propose marriage. I made reservations at the most romantic restaurant I could think of. That night, as we arrived at Chuck-A-Rama . . . (just kidding, it wasn't Chuck-A-Rama).

I brought several small gifts to the restaurant earlier in the day and made arrangements with the waitresses to bring them out one at a time. One of the last gifts was roses and a note. She opened the note and started to read. In my note I told her how hard I had tried to be a good person and how hard I'd tried to find someone like her. I told her how lucky I felt to be with her.

You've probably all heard the saying, "Don't try to find the right one, just try to be the right one." That's really all you can do. In fact, you can say "I love you" to your future husband or wife *tonight* if you want. How? By saying your prayers. By reading your scriptures. By following the gift of the Holy Ghost in your life. Whenever you do those good and righteous things, it's as if you're saying, "I want to be the very best person I can be—not just for me but also for you!"

Elder Jeffrey R. Holland once said, "On your wedding day, the very best gift you can give your eternal companion is your very best self—clean and pure, and worthy of such purity in return" ("Personal Purity," *Ensign,* November 1998, 77). Imagine that. You can start working on your wedding gift to your spouse right now! Because the gift you're going to give is you.

As Kim was reading the note, I noticed that she started to cry. The bottom of the note said, "Look up at me please." When she looked up, I gave her an engagement ring and popped the question, "Will you marry me?" (Young men, I realize you're not going to propose marriage until after your missions, but you might want to remember that it's important when you propose to get your fiancée to cry. The tears in her eyes can serve as a magnifying glass, making the stone in the ring look much larger than it really is. This can affect her answer.)

She said, "Yes," and I did the only thing I could think of—I kissed her. That night as I drove home, I realized that not only did I have a girlfriend, I also had a fiancée! This was one of the first times I really understood Alma 38:12. I've always remembered the advice, "Bridle all your passions," but I'd never finished the sentence. Alma the Younger, who was talking to his son Shiblon in this verse, said, "Bridle all your passions, that ye may be *filled* with love." That is so positive! He didn't say, "Bridle all your passions because those feelings are bad." He said, "Bridle all your passions that ye may be filled with love." This was the first time I thought I knew what Alma meant. I was filled with love.

To make a long story short, one Tuesday morning a few months later I was sitting in the Salt Lake Temple waiting for my bride to meet me so that we could be sealed. Finally she ascended the stairs, beautifully dressed in white. I have always known that the color white represents purity. I didn't realize, however, that there is another meaning, known to the ancient apostles who often used the color in their writings. The color white also means *victory.* Victory over worldly things. There we were, getting married in the temple, "all arrayed in spotless white." We had attended the standards nights, we had learned what the Lord expected of us, and we had made it! We made it to the temple.

In NASCAR a checkered flag is the victory symbol, but for you and me, arriving at the temple dressed in white is our victory symbol of overcoming the world. When I saw Kim coming I was smitten all over again, and as I took her hand, the most wonderful, peaceful feeling came over me. It was as if the Lord was saying, "You made a good choice." (I also thought I heard, "Frankly, I'm surprised you got her.")

We entered the sealing room, surrounded by family, friends, and priesthood power, and Brother Ned Winder sealed us for time and all eternity. Wow, that was something. That night we went to our wedding reception and smiled and shook hands until our teeth got dry and our lips got stuck.

When the reception came to an end, Kim and I ran off to begin our honeymoon, happily and wonderfully naive. We weren't experienced like the world thinks we should be. We hadn't "lived together" or "slept together" or anything like that. We weren't carrying regrets into our new life about immoral mistakes we'd made or dumb things we'd done at parties we shouldn't have attended. We were just a young couple with a clean slate who'd made a commitment to each other that God would help us keep. Once again I thought I knew what Alma meant when he said, "Bridle all your passions, that ye may be filled with love."

But you know what? I was wrong. I mean I was right, but I had no idea how much real love can grow. One day a year or two later, while teaching a Book of Mormon class at Brigham Young University, my cell phone rang. Class had just ended, so I picked up the phone. It was Kim, and she started to cry a little bit and said, "My water broke," which means, "You'd better hurry, I'm in labor."

At 4:54 that afternoon Doctor Brian Woolsey handed me my new little girl. After the nurses cleaned her off, they gave her to Kim. It was one of the coolest things I'd ever seen. She stopped crying and just looked at her Mom. The nurses then took her to the nursery, and after they'd given her a bath and some new clothes, they brought her back. As father, mother, and four-hour-old baby sat together on the bed, I thought, "Okay, Alma, now I *really* get it."

There's no way I can describe it, and I guess that's my point. If you will just bridle your passions now, if you won't push against the fence but will just live your life by the standards the Lord has given you, the day will come when he will fill you with love and happiness that you just can't imagine.

Since then we've had two more children, and the Lord continues to fill our home with love. I am so thankful for the standards. All the happiness that we enjoy now we can trace back to trying to live our lives according to gospel standards. President Boyd K. Packer made this wonderful statement, which inspired the title for this book:

> How foolish is the youth who feels that the Church is a fence around love to keep him out. Oh, youth, if you could know! The requirements of the Church are the highway to love and to happiness, with guardrails securely in place, with guideposts plainly marked, and with help along the way.

How unfortunate to resent counsel and restraint! How fortunate are you who follow the standards of the Church, even if just from sheer obedience or habit! You will find a rapture and a joy fulfilled (*Let Not Your Heart Be Troubled* [Salt Lake City: Bookcraft, 1991], 140).

There's a big difference between a fence that says "KEEP OUT!" and a guardrail that says "BE SAFE!" Satan wants you to think that the standards of the Church are just a bunch of rules to make sure you don't have any fun. He tempts people to say to you, "Man, you can't do anything in your Church!" On the other hand, the Lord wants you to realize that as you bridle your passions *now,* you can have greater joy than you ever thought possible *later.*

Don't let the deceiver deceive you. *Satan* is the enemy of romance, not the Church! *Satan* is the enemy of love and infatuation, not the Church! *Satan* is the enemy of all the joys of wholesome dating and decent relationships, not the Church! Don't get it wrong. Too much is at stake!

In your *For the Strength of Youth* pamphlet, the First Presidency outlines the blessings of keeping the standards:

> We promise that as you keep these standards and live by the truths in the scriptures, you will be able to do your life's work with greater wisdom and skill and bear trials with greater courage. You will have the help of the Holy Ghost. You will feel good about yourself and will be a positive influence in the lives of others. You will be worthy to go to the temple to receive holy ordinances. These blessings and many more can be yours (*For the Strength of Youth,* 2–3).

We've only covered a few topics within the *For the Strength of Youth* pamphlet. The rest I hope you will read on your own. I don't know why they named it *For the Strength of Youth.* They could have called it *How to Have Maximum Happiness* or even

How Not to Totally Mess Up Your Life. I don't know why they called it what they did. I wasn't on the committee. I'm just glad we have it.

This isn't a talk, so I won't close in the name of Jesus Christ. But I've tried to give you solid advice based on the scriptures and the words of the prophets. Just remember, while some may think the standards are about pierced ears and dating, they're about so much more. We sing, "I'll go where you want me to go, . . . I'll say what you want me to say, . . . I'll be what you want me to be" (*Hymns,* no. 270). And do you know what God wants you to be? He wants you to be happy. He really does because he's your Father in Heaven. I'm learning more about Father in Heaven everyday because I have my own children. I love my children tons, and I tell them "No!" every day. To limit their freedom? No. To protect them from consequences.

May you discover by your own obedience the peace that comes from living your life the Lord's way and keeping his Spirit in your life so that you can experience the happiness that only the Lord can give.

INDEX

ABOUT THE AUTHOR

John Bytheway served a mission to the Philippines and later graduated from Brigham Young University. A popular speaker and teacher, John is the author of many best-selling books and audio products, including *Honoring the Priesthood as a Deacon, a Teacher, and a Priest; Five Scriptures that Will Help You Get through Almost Anything;* the *What I Wish I'd Known* series; and *The Best Three Hours of the Week.* John and his wife, Kimberly, are the parents of three children.